THE
AMDEGA
BOOK OF
CONSERVATORIES

THE
AMDEGA
BOOK OF
CONSERVATORIES

DAVID & CHARLES
Newton Abbot · London

This book is dedicated to my wife, Elizabeth, and to my two daughters, Julia and Amanda, without whose encouragement and support the project would not have been completed.

British Library Cataloguing in Publication Data

Bradburn, Anton
    The Amdega book of conservatories.
    1. Garden rooms
    I. Title
    643'.55   SB419

    ISBN 0-7153-8815-0

Typeset by Typesetters (Birmingham) Ltd
Smethwick West Midlands
and printed in Great Britain
by Redwood Burn Limited, Trowbridge, Wilts
for David & Charles Publishers plc
Brunel House   Newton Abbot   Devon

Contents

1
The Conservatory
from the Beginning

Twenty-five years ago McGrath and Frost, co-authors of a substantial volume dealing with the applications of glass in architecture, were recording the demise of the conservatory in these words: '. . . the thought of a conservatory immediately suggests an unvisited adjunct filled with derelict geraniums and gardener's tools.' They were both a little premature. The domestic conservatory was not dead, merely in a state of hibernation so that today nothing could be further from the truth. If we borrow for a moment an idiom from the jargon of marketing science, in terms of its product life cycle the conservatory is positively blooming, and owners are enjoying once again all the benefits of a glass structure whose remarkable history of design and development has roots reaching back a good three hundred years.

Market and consumer surveys reveal that conservatories serve a wide variety of purposes: firstly they provide a setting for general relaxation; then they offer a controllable environment for plant cultivation; for entertaining: and for eating in, especially as a breakfasting area. While many customers who have a nineteenth-century house purchase a traditional conservatory, home owners of houses completed after 1900 tend to favour a conservatory with a more contemporary style. The conservatory that best harmonises with the house itself is of paramount consideration for the majority of purchasers; concerns about its durability, its low maintenance requirements and its degree of energy efficiency all follow closely. Perhaps the most important common finding is that today's conservatory is considered to be an additional room, and is therefore the first choice for those needing more space – when a significantly high proportion of conservatory owners belong to households with four or five resident members it is not difficult to appreciate why this should be so. More than thirteen million homes in the UK are owner-occupied and the size of home ownership is predicted to increase sharply over the next few years – reaching perhaps 90 per cent according to at least one of the more optimistic recent forecasts – if demand is to be met fully. The growing interest in home improvement originates from this substantial degree of home ownership, to the extent that when conservatories became subject to Value Added Tax at 15 per cent in 1984, it in no way depressed the demand for them. Interest in all forms of home improvements, in which home extension is well represented, is increasing all the time; indeed one recent survey quantifies interest as increasing at the rate of nine per cent per annum, a conclusion which is reflected in the fact that home improvement loans averaging around £3,500 each were made to more than 100,000 of its borrowers by just one leading building society in the year 1984 to 1985 – and this was an increase of some £40 million on the previous year. So the message up to the mid-eighties has unquestionably been one of not moving to a bigger home, but of improving and enlarging the present one.

A *conservatory provides extra living space as well as a beautiful extension to your home. An octagonal ended conservatory containing special roof glass and high side framing* (see interior pp 6–7)

9

The Government's Green Paper of 1985 assessing trends in home improvements, as completed by both owners and tenants, put the total size of the market at a staggering £7,500 million a year. Of this, around £2,000 million was estimated to have been spent on all forms of home extensions. Within this latter category conservatories represented a mere 0.5 per cent, or £12 million. By 1987 the conservatory market had grown to a staggering £48 million and it is estimated this will rise to between £60 million and £70 million in 1988. Amdega currently dominate the 'tailor-made' end of the market and Banbury Homes & Gardens Ltd the volume end, between them taking more than a third of the total market in roughly equal proportions. When the cost per room in an average house comes out at something like £4,000, a conservatory – with its dry construction methods – is quickly appreciated as an efficient and cost-effective way of achieving additional space.

However, the history of today's conservatory is inseparable from the development of horticultural science: this could be said to have its origins in mid-sixteenth-century Italy at the height of the Renaissance when the world's first botanic gardens were established in Pisa, followed closely by those of Florence, Padua, and by Bologna

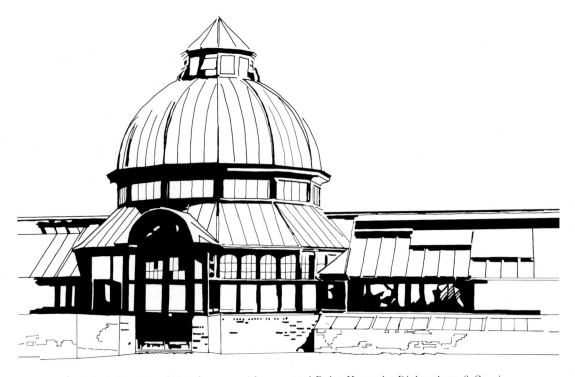

Fig 1 A range of glasshouses with a central Palm House by Richardson & Co for S Japhet Esq of Tinivelli, Caterham. The impressive structure was in teak wood with teak wood Parisian lath blinds across the roof spans

only a little later. It was to be a further eighty years or so before England could record a botanic garden on her native soil, despite the interest in horticulture that had been stimulated by the great Elizabethan explorers and the discovery of many previously unknown plant species. The Earl of Danby takes credit for establishing in 1621 this nation's first botanic garden on land belonging to the University of Oxford. Unfortunately England's maritime climate was, and is, barely comparable to the native climes of these imported species and consequently they rarely survived. English winters were the most destructive, of course. It was not until late in the seventeenth century that Jacob Bobart, in his capacity as keeper of these same Oxford botanic gardens, attempted a solution to the problem of overwintering imported species. Bobart himself had been instrumental in securing a range of plant specimens that he was anxious should not be lost to the winter cold. He designed what might be regarded as a prototype conservatory. With its three windows allowing only restricted amounts of light inside the building, and with an open brazier giving out plant-poisoning fumes as well as life-preserving heat, Bobart's wintering shed was crude by modern standards. But taken in its historical context it marked a very significant achievement and initiated a new era in horticultural progress. However, there was still a very long way to go before the conservatory would begin to emerge in its more familiar form. Innovations spread fairly quickly and within a year or two a structure not dissimilar from Bobart's appeared in the Apothecaries' Garden in Chelsea, although by all accounts it may have been rather more sophisticated than the original.

The problems of keeping rare plant specimens alive from one summer to the next provoked a dissatisfaction not far removed from the growing discontent with the climate of northern Europe in general, perceived by many to be turning colder by degrees. Only a fortunate few, in the affluent ranks of the monarchy and nobility, were in any position to afford a solution. Opinions remain divided as to the primary function of the orangeries that were being built as the answer to the progressively deteriorating climate. Some writers maintain that the orangeries built in the gardens of English palaces and grand country houses were intended to serve as hot houses for the preservation of the citrus bushes so fashionable by the time of Restoration high society. Equally, other writers argue that these citrus bushes were not so much symbolic of conspicuous wealth, but more a form of interior decoration in what were actually detached banqueting and summer supper halls located in their garden settings away from the main house. These various halls, generically referred to as orangeries, served then as convenient storage spaces for citrus, pineapple and any other exotic plants during the winter months, and while there may have been no suppers or banquets during the winter

Interior of a winter garden on the home of J Kirkley Esq by Richardson & Co to a design by J H Morton architect.

season the orangery did continue to provide a pleasant, warm, citrus-scented recreational environment for the ladies of the household to enjoy during the day. Lending weight to this latter opinion is the evidence provided by the example of Queen Anne, for whose benefit the architects Wren, Vanbrugh and Hawksmoor collaborated in 1704 to design the Kensington Palace orangery which was used as both a supper house in summer and an indoor promenade in winter.

Orangeries appeared with increasing frequency from the beginning of the eighteenth century onwards: for example, the orangery at Chatsworth was completed in 1700 for the first Duke of Devonshire, and they were built in the prevailing architectural style, the excessively decorative Baroque predominating. Although the first glazed conservatory is recorded in Heidelberg earlier in the seventeenth century, these structures were not yet the province of the gardener; they remained merely decorative additions to the formal grounds and took little or no account of any horticultural requirements. As the century progressed, however, the orangery *per se* gradually became less fashionable until by the 1750s citrus bushes were being supplanted by other exotic species. These proved even less hardy. Unlike the orange and lemon bushes which were moved outdoors during the summer months, these other, more delicate species, demanded a permanent indoor habitat for their continued survival. The successful cultivation of these plants led to a better understanding of horticultural science, particularly as success was found to depend upon the inter-relationship of those fundamental variables, heating, lighting and ventilation. As a direct result the design of orangeries was modified and improved considerably. Significantly Kew Gardens were founded in 1761 with the construction of an orangery for Augusta, the dowager Princess of Wales. The last quarter of the eighteenth century saw the orangery becoming less architectural and more horticultural as façades featured more windows. At first only south-facing elevations were glazed, but eventually east and west elevations as well as roofs were glazed too. One of England's foremost landscape gardeners, Humphrey Repton, was active in promoting glazed roofs in orangeries. Repton had been quick to realise the importance of roof lighting for healthy plant growth, and having applied this hypothesis, his reward was in seeing a steady increase in the successful cultivation of plant varieties that by far superseded the ubiquitous citrus to include ericas, myrtles and geraniums. By the 1790s heating systems were becoming much more sophisticated as well, as it was realised that fumes from direct open fires were harmful to plants. One of the first indirect heating systems, using hot water, was installed in the Jardin des Plantes in Paris, whilst elsewhere ducted warm air was the preferred method of heating.

Once effective artificial heating systems were established, the art of conserving plants within a glass environment developed very rapidly. While water, heat and air became increasingly easy to control, light remained a problem, and shortage of light in the English winters meant that successful conservatories needed as much glass as possible to permit maximum penetration all year round.

'The conservatory,' wrote the architect John Papworth, 'is a glass building which affords protection to rare and exotic plants solely for the reason of display.' Papworth thereby distinguished the conservatory from its more utilitarian cousin, the greenhouse, and settled at the same time the controversy about whether a conservatory could only be so called if it were a free-standing structure. Probably because of his training Papworth looked first at the function of the building, considering its form to be a secondary issue. The purpose of the building would determine its form and would also influence the kind of materials used in its construction. Whether the conservatory was a free-standing structure or one integrated into the fabric of the house itself was no longer relevant. Papworth certainly resolved the issue for Humphrey Repton, who had been exhibiting considerable indecision on the matter. In 1803 Repton had been one of the strongest advocates for the ideal conservatory to be an independent building, yet only twelve years later he was advising with equal conviction that conservatories should be connected to the house – preferably by means of a porch or short corridor. Also in 1803, when

An alternative to a finish in white is natural wood treated with cedar-stain.

Repton was publishing his *Observations on the Theory and Practice of Landscape Gardening*, Joseph Paxton was born, the man who was to become the most influential figure in the field of conservatory design and construction.

Paxton left his Bedfordshire farming family to take up a gardening post with the Royal Horticultural Society in Chiswick at nineteen years of age. Within four years he had come to the notice of the sixth Duke of Devonshire, who employed him as head gardener at Chatsworth House from 1826 onwards. At about this time, the third Duke of Northumberland was no doubt delighting in the completion of his magnificent conservatory at Syon House. Architect designed by Charles Fowler, Syon Plant House was a superb example of a stonebuilt conservatory whose environment was dedicated to plants. Almost seven years in the building, the Plant House set out to recreate a jungle habitat which included exotic wild birds and other small animals in addition to the plants themselves. It has often been suggested that this building represented the duke's attempt to re-create the Garden of Eden. However that may have been, the Plant

House was of major significance because it incorporated some of the most up-to-date scientific principles developed by another leading pioneer of conservatory design – John Claudius Loudon. Loudon had been experimenting with his own conservatory prototype at his home in Bayswater. One of his main concerns was to find out the optimum angle at which panes of glass should be inclined to the sun, so as to allow maximum penetration by its rays and consequently achieve the highest levels of light within the building for the benefit of the plants.

First Anderson, then Knight had presented research papers to the Horticultural Society in 1809 dealing with improved angling of glass roofs. Thomas Knight even went so far as to calculate that correctly angled glass would improve the flavour of grapes on the vine, or produce a more perfect peach in a conservatory at Russian latitudes than on an Italian peach tree out in the open air. But it was Sir George Mackenzie who in 1815 discovered that the optimum form for sunlight penetration is a hemisphere. While confirming Mackenzie's findings, Loudon's experiments went much further, advancing the design of the conservatory very considerably. Realising that plant houses need bevelled surfaces to dispel moisture that would otherwise collect and cause decay, Loudon devised a moulded wrought-iron sash bar capable of replacing its wooden counterpart. Not only did this new design help improve curvilinear glass structures, but it was also capable of spanning much larger areas. As well as the sash bar Loudon also worked to improve conservatory ventilation, and perfected an automatic louvred system connected by levers and pulleys, and controlled by a thermostat that had only recently been invented by James Kewley in 1816. In addition to this, Loudon evolved the ridge-and-furrow system of roof design that was later to be used so successfully by Paxton at Chatsworth. Having presented his ideas to the Horticultural Society in 1816, conservatory builders like W. G. and D. Bailey were quick to incorporate them into new schemes. In the case of the Baileys, Loudon's ideas quickly found their way into the design for a 'vinery and pineapple pit' commissioned in Somerset: but by far the most outstanding in this new generation of conservatories designed on Loudon principles, is considered to have been the one erected for Mrs Beaumont at Bretton Hall near Wakefield in 1827. Although this was to be sold at auction on her death only five years later, then dismantled and removed, Mrs Beaumont's conservatory is regarded as the forerunner of those subsequently built at Kew, Chiswick and at Chatsworth. It

OVERLEAF

This double octagonal conservatory complements the design of the house perfectly and makes an ideal place for some quiet reading.

certainly featured prominently in Loudon's *Encyclopaedia of Cottage, Farm and Villa Architecture* published in 1833.

However by 1838, despite the Duke of Northumberland's Syon Plant House, architectural conservatories had fallen out of favour. On a point of interest, Amdega must at one time have been involved with extensions to, or the refurbishment of, the Syon conservatory complex. Amdega, formerly Richardsons of Darlington and London Belgravia, still have plans in their archives of the duke's magnificent Plant House although there is no accompanying record of quite what the firm's involvement may have been. But Richardsons could not have been associated with the original building project, as W. Richardson & Company was established almost half a century afterwards in 1874 to cater for the booming market in domestic conservatories at that time. However, there is a second company, still actively trading today but in modern rather than traditional conservatories, which was first heard of at about the time of the Syon Plant House's completion. The antecedents of Crittal Warmlife can be traced back to the Thomas Clark Company of Birmingham, responsible for a Camelia Hall at Wollaton House in Nottingham as early as 1823. This firm later became Hopes, then Crittal–Hope and eventually Crittal Warmlife.

The evolution of the conservatory continued as architectural fashion gave way to the needs of the gardener and the horticulturist. Probably the best example of the horticultural conservatory was the Great Conservatory at Chatsworth designed by Joseph Paxton, which was completed in 1840. The Great Conservatory made use of cast-iron pillars for its structural support, but it was mainly built of wood. The structure enclosed an area of 3,630sq yd (3,034sq m), and, standing 65ft (13.75m) high, it cost the Duke of Devonshire just a little more than £33,000 to complete. Paxton designed the Great Conservatory so that visitors could drive through its main aisle in an open carriage, which Queen Victoria actually did in 1848, or promenade on its cast-iron mezzanine gallery. This Paxton conservatory demonstrated the measure of environmental control that could now be exercised by the Victorian gardener. The Great Conservatory had eight boilers tucked away in its basements, heating water which was conducted along 7 miles (11.2km) of 4in (10cm) diameter pipework running around its interior. So vast was the consumption of fuel it was almost on an industrial scale, with coke being moved into the boilerhouse by means of a special tramway.

Ironically, the Great Conservatory was almost outdated before its completion, because in using mainly wood for its construction Paxton had not adopted the most modern building material available to him. While wood invested his Great Conservatory with a lightness that contrasted with the sense of mass that had characterised those earlier architectural examples, it did not have the load-bearing qualities of cast iron nor its durability. The introduction of both wrought and cast iron, most particularly the latter, to conservatory construction meant that very large areas could be spanned with ease. Once glass technology caught up with cast-iron processing, and once glass prices had fallen dramatically following the abolition of the glass tax, the way was clear for someone to design and build a truly spectacular conservatory that would demonstrate the advantages of a structural framework with glass curtain walls.

It remained to Joseph Paxton, later Sir Joseph, to demonstrate most convincingly just how effective iron and glass structures could be. Eleven years after his notable achievement at Chatsworth, and only three years after Victoria's visit to his Great Conservatory, Paxton was to submit the renowned 'blotting paper sketch' for what was to become the Crystal Palace, to house Prince Albert's masterly concept, the Great Exhibition of 1851. Paxton's successful submission of this design immediately polarised opinion and generated considerable acrimony among the other 245 competitors, many of them architects, whose schemes had already been rejected by the Exhibition's selection panel. Despite its prodigious scale the Crystal Palace was not architectural by the standards of the time – it was constructional, relying on engineering principles, and it marked the most significant advance in system building based as it was on the use

Fig 2 The Preston Hall conservatory intended for use as a Winter Garden – was constructed of teak wood and painted in white

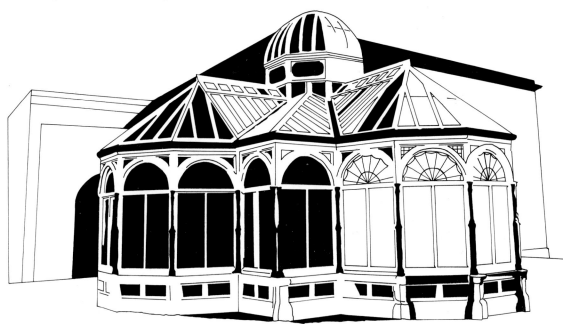

of prefabricated standard modules. This structure was the synthesis of several of Paxton's own earlier experiments at Chatsworth – the use of ridge-and-furrow roofing, for example – but it also incorporated ideas pioneered by Loudon, Mackenzie, Knight, Anderson and not least by Abraham Darby the Third of Coalbrookdale in Shropshire. The fact that Paxton's design, based on previous work for the Victoria Regia Lily House at Chatsworth in 1849, was accepted was probably due to two separate influences: firstly, the time available to complete an appropriate building to house the Great Exhibition had become almost impossibly foreshortened as a result of the delays occasioned by the earlier rejections of so many alternative proposals. Secondly was the masterly way a public relations campaign was mounted by Paxton, intended to marshal public opinion behind his own submission. While the selection panel was still considering his submission Paxton arranged to have it published in the *Illustrated London News*. As a direct result, public interest was stimulated to such an extent that the committee was left with virtually no alternative but to give way to public pressure and accept the Paxton plan.

Paxton's resolution of this major design problem was elegant in its simplicity. He conceived the Crystal Palace as the ultimate functional structure. However, because Paxton was still essentially a gardener rather than a trained engineer, all the design calculations were executed by the firm of Charles Fox. The specifications in the design of the Crystal Palace are still awe-inspiring even by today's standards. Central to the design was the 24ft (7.315m) module, a whole series of which could be mass-produced at the foundry, then bolted together and erected on site at Hyde Park to form a cruciform framework which would subsequently be fully glazed. The structure was 2,000ft (609.6m) long, 408ft (127m) wide and provided 33 million cu ft (93,445cu m) of space. Its roof area covered 17½ acres (7.07 hectares), and together with its walls the structure required 250,000 panes of glass that were supported on 4,500 tons of ironwork. Outside, some 24 miles (38.6km) of guttering carried away excess surface rainwater, while inside the Crystal Palace maintained an optimum temperature by means of 22 boilers, each with the capacity for heating 5,500 gallons (24,750 litres) of water circulating around 55 miles (88.5km) of piping. All of this took the remarkably short time of just sixteen months to complete, making the Crystal Palace ready to meet its opening deadline of 1 May 1851, housing the very successful Great Exhibition which ran for twenty consecutive weeks. Once the Exhibition closed the Crystal Palace was purchased by a company formed especially for the purpose, with Paxton as one of its principals, disassembled and transported to a new site at Sydenham. Once there it was re-erected as what nowadays would be described as a leisure complex, and contained a 4,000-seat concert

A domestic conservatory erected for J Nicholson Esq of Wheatfield, Head-ingley, Leeds. It was manufactured by Richardson & Co to a design from the architect T Butler Wilson of Leeds. A particularly interesting detail is the arch roof span to the front and side elevations that deliberately echo features of the Crystal Palace.

auditorium, restaurants, exhibition areas, and by no means least – a conservatory. Unfortunately this magnificent example of Victorian ingenuity was destroyed by fire on 30 November 1936.

The significance of Paxton's Crystal Palace and the impetus it gave to popularising the domestic conservatory cannot be understated. Almost everyone wanted his own personal version of the Crystal Palace. Perhaps the one individual who came closer to achieving this than anyone else was Josiah Nicholson of Leeds who engaged the services of an architectural practice – T. B. Wilson – to design him a domestic conservatory with very strong references to the Crystal Palace. The structure was built by Richardson & Company of Darlington in 1892 and the barrel-vaulted curvilinear roof is a carefully re-scaled version of the Crystal Palace original. However, Paxton's building was not in itself innovatory. Rather his genius was in bringing together several ideas that had already been perfected singly elsewhere and by others. Then there is the inescapable fact, as pointed out by McGrath and Frost, that the Crystal Palace was not so much a conservatory of plants but rather of an era. Writing of achievements in dedicated conservatory design proper, these co-authors point instead to the Palm House at Kew that used only 360,000sq ft (32,400sq m) of glass to cover a structure 360ft (109.4m) long by 100ft (30.4m) wide and 66ft (20.05m) high. It was of modest proportions compared to the Crystal Palace and cost barely £30,000. Curiously there is some discrepancy between McGrath and Frost on the one hand and James Curl on the other. According to the former, Kew's Palm House was completed fifteen years after the Great Exhibition, but Curl writes that the Kew Gardens actually pre-dated the Crystal Palace by some three years. What is certain is that designer Richard Turner collaborated with architect Decimus Burton to produce an outstandingly fine glass and cast-iron structure. Turner's expertise lay in his ability to design cast-iron frameworks, and he had previously worked with architect Sir Charles Lanyon on the Belfast Palm House which had opened in 1839. Turner's refinement of system-building techniques, and their application to conservatories, was itself developed from earlier innovations in the use of prefabricated components – these had been introduced more than sixty years previously by Abraham Darby at Coalbrookdale when he successfully pioneered the engineering and construction of the Iron Bridge spanning the Severn gorge using cast-iron sections bolted together. Cast iron was shunned as being not respectable enough for use in domestic structures, until Nash used it in building the Brighton Pavilion for the Prince Regent in 1821. Thirty years later cast iron's respectability was publicly confirmed in the commissioning of the Crystal Palace. Spurred on by his success in Belfast and at Kew, Richard Turner was precocious enough to submit a design of his own, without benefit of architect collaboration, to house the Great Exhibition. 'It only resembled,' writes Curl, 'a cross between a railway terminus and a cathedral with a palm house sitting on top.' Consequently it was consigned to join the other 244 rejections. Despite this particular disappointment for Turner, nothing can detract from his earlier successes.

The large, public conservatories like Belfast, Kew and others often served a double purpose: gardening and leisure. Certainly there was a vogue for escapism engendered by the sense of romanticism which pervaded Victorian society, and this was reflected in the decorative style. Nor was this solely confined to English shores. Neumann, as Director of the Botanic Gardens in Paris, suggested irregular tracery be incorporated into wrought-iron sash bars to simulate the pattern of light piercing typical jungle foliage. Loudon went even further and encouraged the employment of individuals recruited from indigenous jungle races to serve as gardeners in these conservatories, thereby further promoting the illusion of a jungle environment. Beside all this

OPPOSITE

Fig 3 Part of the interior of the Preston Hall Winter Garden conservatory recently refurbished and now open for public enjoyment

however, there was a commercial ethic operating too. In these spacious conservatories, with their controllable environments, could be studied a wide range of plants – banana, rubber, coffee, cotton and cocoa – each with its own particular significance for a section of the national economy. Harnessing illusion and reality together these large Palm Houses remained open for the benefit of the public all year round, and in time came to be known as 'winter gardens'. Paris had its Jardin d'Hiver on the Champs Elyseés from 1847; Berlin's winter gardens were said to spring from the close of the Napoleonic Wars. In Russia one of the finest examples was reckoned to be at the Taurida Palace of Potemkin in St Petersburg, while Poland too boasted an exceptional winter garden in the form of a large conservatory on the property of one Prince Poniatowski. Other smaller public conservatories were specifically designed to provide a habitat for the *Victoria regia* lily that had become increasingly fashionable from the year of Victoria's coronation when the first specimens arrived in England. They did not thrive, and again it remained to Joseph Paxton to devise the ideal environment in which the lilies would flourish. The design for his heated water tank was completed in 1849. The first small lily specimen, less than 12in (30.4cm) in diameter, was carefully installed in early August that same year. Within seven weeks it had grown to a diameter of 42in (105cm) and only five weeks later England recorded its first home-grown *Victoria regia* bloom. Before long, purpose-designed conservatories, like the charming Lily House in Leyden (1870), were appearing to grace botanical gardens all over Europe.

The interest in conservatories became almost as intense as the railway mania of the 1840s. Scores of periodicals appeared – 'Floral World' for example – to cater for conservatory enthusiasts. At the domestic level conservatories became, as Alan Toogood remarks, an essential part of the nineteenth century's middle class social fabric where guests could be entertained amid exotic flora. Conservatories functioned as dining rooms, music rooms, even billiard rooms; many became essentially a female domain. Apart from the intrinsic pleasure to be derived from such surroundings, there was a keen sense of social rivalry not entirely dissimilar from the status rivalry apparent among the nobility in the high period of the orangery. This aside, the rise and rise of the domestic conservatory is attributable to several factors. Sustained industrial success had resulted in the rise of an affluent middle class with leisure time to be enjoyed, which presented a growing market and the possibility of further conservatory sales. Coincidentally the cost of glass had plummeted so that instead of being expensive, it had become one of the least costly of building materials. Following the success of the Crystal Palace, cast iron had become socially acceptable, and prefabricated building systems meant conservatories could be popularly priced to take advantage of this substantial market. One of the major advantages of using standardised components was design flexibility, and this meant that conservatories could be adapted to meet the specific requirements of locations ranging from rooftops and balconies to porches and corridors. Consequently attached domestic conservatories, although on a modest scale compared with their more noble, detached counterparts, became an essential addition to the Victorian house – probably nowhere more so than in fashionable Belgravia where Richardson & Company had its London base. Although conservatories were not entirely successful in industrialised urban areas, particularly on rooftop sites, elsewhere in the non-industrial cities they maintained their popularity well into the Edwardian era.

What really brought the first life-cycle of the conservatory to a close was a combination of several different factors working together over a period of time. At the beginning of the Edwardian period William Robinson published his acclaimed volume entitled *The English Flower Garden*. Robinson's ideal was the English cottage garden and it presaged a return to real gardening outdoors thereby hastening a decline of interest in artificial gardening under glass. Fuel rationing introduced in World War I caused an unspecified number of conservatory plant collections to die from lack of heat. After the War

The horse drawn carriage may have been progressively replaced by the horseless carriage, but the Richardson structure was still favoured as a garage. This glass roof was erected over a former stable yard at the home of Mrs Illingworth, Lady Royde Hall near Bradford.

they were simply never replaced. That great army of poorly remunerated, unseen domestic servants, gardeners and handymen, on whose labours the successful maintenance of many a conservatory had principally depended, had been severely reduced by the War. A good many had become casualties of it; others had been lured away from domestic service forever by the higher wages of the factories. An age of confidence, of luxury and elegance was crumbling, was coming to a close, and in the scale of domestic priorities now facing the masters and mistresses of many a household for the first time the conservatory barely signified. Symbolic of this profound change in the social fabric was the destruction of two outstanding Paxton structures. His Great Conservatory at Chatsworth finally succumbed to the explosive charges of the demolition contractors between the Wars – its destruction was occasioned mainly by escalating costs in maintenance associated with severe problems in the conservatory's putty glazing. Only a few years later the Crystal Palace was accidentally destroyed by fire. The gradual decline in the remaining stock of English conservatories was precipitated by the outbreak of World War II; when peace was eventually restored more than five years later, interest in conservatories had all but withered away. Added to this, a new social postwar era was emerging, characterised by a lack of interest in gardening generally, especially among the younger generation. As the austerity years of the late forties and early fifties faded away and as rationing ended, the pace of life began to quicken, and expectations to rise, culminating in Harold Macmillan's pronouncement that the British nation had 'never had it so good'. Eventually higher earnings stimulated consumerism and coupled with improved physical communications – especially low-cost mass transport systems – there was a demand for new forms of recreation and entertainment outside the home.

As the market for domestic conservatories went into recession from the early years of this century onwards, so a number of those companies that had established themselves during the boom years were to go out of business. Others, like W. Richardson & Company who had previously promoted themselves as suppliers of horticultural buildings to the nobility and gentry, clung on tenaciously, helped by the diversity of what they were able to manufacture and supply. Richardsons, for example, offered a huge range of bespoke products, from the most decorative of winter gardens to the plainest and smallest amateur's greenhouse. The company also manufactured summer houses, bandstands, garages, verandahs and porches. Indeed, even a cursory glance at one edition of the firm's catalogue published during the inter-war years – priced then at 2/6d (12½p) – readily demonstrates that Richardsons were concerned not merely with structures, but also with the way they functioned. Consequently this particular horticultural engineering enterprise could provide heating and ventilation equipment as well as fixtures and fittings for both inside and outdoor use. The company's comprehensive catalogue offered everything from a veritable juggernaut of a heating system powered by the Robin Hood Senior boiler at £95, right down to the smallest socket or spigot with a retail value of no more than a few pennies.

Domestic conservatory design continued to be the subject of research and development, despite depressed market conditions, leading to such improvements as dry glazing to replace puttied glazing, and the introduction of new materials like aluminium in place of cast iron or wood. There were even new companies entering the field, the most notable of which was the company now known as Banbury Homes & Gardens Limited. However, the future still looked bleak. The renaissance of the domestic conservatory did not get under-way until the early 1970s. Writing about the Grand Conservatories some ten years ago John Hix makes the point that they could only flourish in an age of affluence. Now, looking back from our present standpoint in the mid-1980s, it seems not unreasonable to regard the affluence of the sixties as the prime cause of renewed interest in domestic conservatories. The effect, though, has since been twofold. When money was more readily available in the years prior to the present recession, house prices began to spiral upwards at an ever-increasing rate; anyone wanting more living space could either move to a larger property or extend an existing home. Of these two alter-natives the second still remains the least expensive, and in seeking to increase domestic space home owners continue to opt for the more cost-effective solution that adding a conservatory represents. Other home owners are less concerned with increasing domestic space, and add a conservatory as a games room housing the pool table perhaps, to roof the swimming pool, as a location for a whirlpool bath, as some-where to site a cocktail bar for entertaining guests, to serve as a paint-ing studio or craft workshop. One recent survey reveals that 60 per cent of owners do still keep plants in their conservatories but only as a secondary consideration. The structure is in fact regarded as sufficiently adaptable to meet an ever-increasing catalogue of lifestyle requirements.

A conservatory provides an extension into the garden

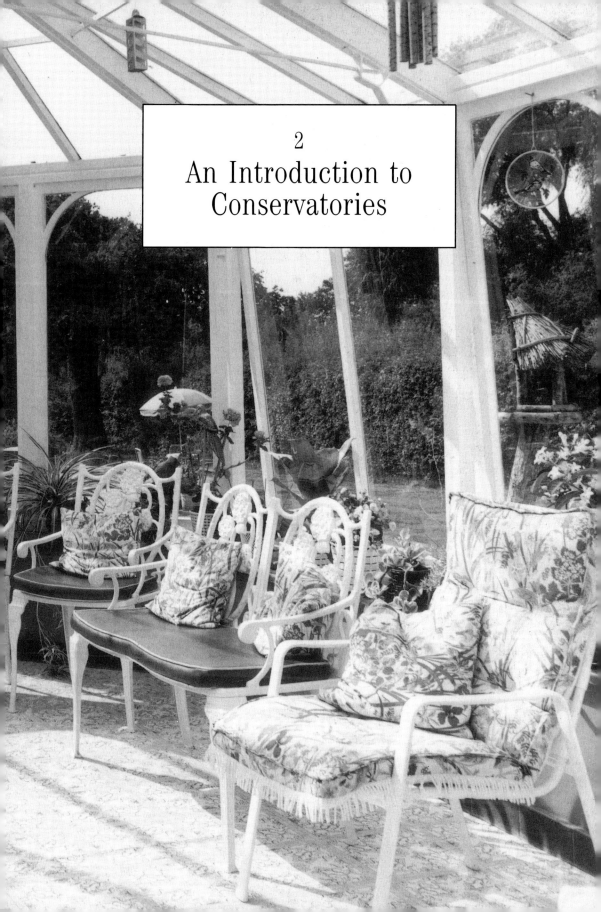

2
An Introduction to Conservatories

A conservatory is about as close as it is possible to come to alfresco living; it extends your home right into your garden. It allows the best of the British climate to be enjoyed, while providing comfortable shelter from the worst of it. The manufacturers' glossy sales brochures will tell you that a conservatory can be designed to suit any lifestyle – that such structures are truly spaces for all seasons. While some of what these brochures claim may be taken with the proverbial pinch of salt, it certainly does not make what the manufacturers say in this particular respect any the less true.

A conservatory may begin as no more than a stack of seasoned timber, or miles of unglamorous aluminium extrusions, but the leading manufacturers between them can offer a choice of styles and sizes that will enhance virtually any home or commercial building. The conservatory can also be a very practical investment. In his book *Home Extensions & Conservatories* David Fisher explains how these structures can function as sources of 'free heat' owing to their ability to absorb and trap solar energy, which can subsequently be induced to circulate within adjacent domestic spaces. Fisher goes on to describe a heat pump system based on a principle not unlike the now familiar solar panels frequently seen located on house roofs.

In addition to the unexpected gain of 'free' energy, other more tangible benefits may be anticipated following the acquisition of a conservatory. There is, for example, the idea of 'added value' that manufacturers frequently apply to a wide range of goods: the idea is that by taking a basic material and putting it through a number of simple processes the original material is transformed into a product of much higher value. Where the conservatory is concerned the existing property may be considered as the basic product into which a smaller structure is integrated. The market value of the original house is frequently found to be enhanced by the addition of a conservatory which improves the property's overall value by much more than the purchase price of the added structure.

As well as the increase in value conferred by the addition of a conservatory, a further benefit is the immediate increase in domestic space which may either be used in a functional way – serving as a dining space sited adjacent to a kitchen, for instance – or used less frequently perhaps and therefore fulfilling an essentially more decorative, even spiritual purpose. Whether it is built to meet more functional or more aesthetic needs, a conservatory can appeal equally to the more rational values of the convivial personality as well as to the emotional needs of the more creative individual. And because on completion of a conservatory project new space is immediately and permanently available the structure can quickly rekindle enjoyment of the domestic environment.

Yet another benefit is the cost advantage on the purchase price of a conservatory by the careful avoidance of value added tax. The VAT

The octagonal conservatory complements this bungalow perfectly.

A standard octagonal conservatory in a white finish.

rules applying to conservatories are by no means easy to understand, but at the beginning of 1987 the following guidelines in respect of new homes and listed buildings were operating: First the distinction has to be made between goods and service. Where a service is supplied, like the erection of a conservatory, VAT does not always have to be charged as long as both materials and service are provided by the same supplier. Thus when a purchaser specifies both the supply and erection of a conservatory to a manufacturer then the manufacturer's subsequent invoice may be zero rated for VAT purposes thus saving 15 per cent for some customers. But it must be emphasised firstly that this only applies to owners of new houses, or Grade One or Two listed buildings; and also that this VAT legislation may only be exploited in this way where the order includes both supply and erection. If a customer's order specifies only the supply of a conservatory then VAT must be charged. This is one good reason for not attempting a DIY approach to installing a conservatory. It also follows that in particular circumstances a 'cash and carry' aluminium conservatory may turn out to be less of a bargain than it seemed.

Even this apparent concession, though, still requires that owners of new houses must supply VAT officers with appropriate plans and elevations accompanied by a written undertaking that occupation will not take place before the whole building – including the conservatory – is completed. Owners of listed buildings must be able to supply a copy of their local authority's Listed Building Consent so that VAT officers can agree a zero-rated invoice from the conservatory manufacturer. It should also be noted that any property referred to as a Grade Three listed building does not qualify for a zero-rated invoice. In addition, a free-standing design of conservatory does not qualify for a zero-rated invoice under any circumstances.

This is the basic outline of the VAT position, and while it may seem somewhat complex, it has given rise to several imaginative schemes originated by manufacturers like Amdega by means of which payment of VAT may be circumvented. Basically these schemes encourage intending purchasers to nominate their own VAT-registered builders to supply and erect their conservatories. Where a new dwelling is to be occupied in the future it is possible for the owners to nominate themselves as their own builders. In both instances the builder will be charged VAT by the manufacturer, but will subsequently be able to reclaim the tax through the normal procedures. The nominated builder is then able to zero rate a VAT invoice to his client for the service he has supplied, which of course

OPPOSITE

Internal view of an Amdega designed double lean-to conservatory complete with MSH/MSR window sashes, dentil moulding, ridge casting, and a special cartwheel feature in the gable end.

includes the labour cost involved and the materials (the conservatory itself in this case) used in carrying out the service.

One further refinement to the fundamental scheme outlined above involves placing an order direct to a manufacturer who operates both a supply and an erection service, while undertaking a DIY or sub-contracting approach for the installation of the necessary ground-work. Some structures – mainly the aluminium ones – will have 'instant' bases, or require only minimal groundwork preparation. However, the majority of timber conservatories will require the careful construction of some form of foundation. Unfortunately specifications for these bases vary from one local authority to another so it is not possible to be precise in case the recommendations are followed slavishly only to prove unacceptable on completion. What can be said, however, is that whether a solid concrete raft is put in, or whether brickwork dwarf walls are built up on concrete footings, the base must be flat, level, square, and at right angles to the wall of the property otherwise difficulties will be encountered with the sub-sequent assembly and glazing.

The conservatory should be conceived of as both a space for all seasons as well as a space for virtually all reasons. In the course of a single day one of these structures might serve as a breakfast room, an auditorium for listening to music, a poolside changing room (when fitted with appropriate blinds!) or somewhere to cool off after a vigorous game of tennis. It might enclose anything from a whirlpool bath to a swimming pool; might provide playing space for children or teenagers – with pool or table-tennis tables. A conservatory readily becomes a painting studio, or craft workshop; it can make a charming summer house, an ideal place for some quiet reading. Then in the evening it offers an appealing place to dine or to take cocktails or coffee with family and friends.

Conservatories are either lean-to or free-standing structures, and can be rectangular, octagonal, hard-edged or curvilinear, symmetrical or asymmetrical in form. While their setting is mainly domestic, they are being used increasingly in commercial situations. Many a public house now has its conservatory where food catering is offered, for example, and they have been observed as a feature of motorway catering establishments as well. They are offices, hair salons, tea rooms. However, these are examples of innovative use not yet commonplace – even so they do indicate the growing range of possibilities offered by a conservatory that is far removed from its original purpose as a space in which to cultivate and enjoy a wide variety of plants from season to season.

OPPOSITE

A semi-detached Edwardian villa with a rare example of a detatched conservatory.

A conservatory might serve as a breakfast room or house a swimming pool
NORTHERN PHOTOGRAPHIC SERVICES

Differences in marketing strategy and which particular part of the market is targeted are fundamentals when distinguishing one conservatory manufacturer from another, as are the materials and the differing production methods they employ. No two manufacturers appear to operate in precisely the same way, but the use of an agent network is general to those firms offering aluminium conservatories, as distinct from timber alternatives. Frequently an agent is also an authorised dealer for the particular product, and again it is not uncommon for an authorised dealer to be a garden centre. Bickerdikes Garden Centres in Bedfordshire and Cambridgeshire are typical examples, where a range of aluminium conservatories produced by several leading firms will be erected fully glazed, partly furnished and on display in an appropriate setting. Banbury Homes & Gardens Limited have developed this strategy to the full in recent years with a nationwide network of around fifty Display Centres – many of them within garden centres – from which they sell not only their own range of cedar conservatories, but also a vast selection of aluminium models from other leading manufacturers; in fact, the widest selection of conservatories available from any single source of supply. The benefit to the customer in this approach to sales and marketing is that these structures may be seen in three dimensions and compared at first hand. An additional bonus is that the expertise of the dealer can be tapped to provide additional advice about appropriate plants, furnishings, flooring, and a host of other useful details connected with conservatory accessories.

Although there will be notable exceptions of course, suitability of style is another important principle that differentiates the manufacturer working in the more natural material of timber from the company offering an aluminium product. Those timber conservatories with a distinctively Victorian or Edwardian style about them are probably more suited to houses built prior to 1920 – to take a very arbitrary date – while metal-framed structures seem to lend themselves more readily to houses built during the inter-war years and post-1945. Quite often it is details such as the metal casements in houses typical of the so-called international style that suggest the aluminium conservatory as the more appropriate addition. Sometimes it is simply that modern homes emphasise practicality, and seem to eschew decorative detail, and provoke a hard-edged functionalist architecture that can be more closely associated with the spirit of the machine age. On the whole, the form of the aluminium conservatory displays a similarly functional, machine-age personality that derives from the nature of the material itself, from the production process of component parts and the methods of assembly.

Ultimately, it is very important to feel truly at home with a conservatory whatever type is eventually chosen to meet particular requirements. This living relationship can best be achieved by

In the evening a conservatory offers an appealing place to dine, take cocktails or coffee with friends

NORTHERN PHOTOGRAPHIC SERVICES

A conservatory has been added to The Old Horse pub in the centre of Leicester.

considering carefully all the possibilities prior to purchasing; the purchaser must therefore consult as much appropriate information as possible so as to enable the most satisfactory choice to be made. The purpose of this book is to help with initial decision-making, and to act as a guide to the long-term enjoyment of a conservatory.

Making decisions about purchasing a conservatory is no easy matter, but it can be facilitated by making some kind of comparison between the majors in conservatory manufacturing. A wide-ranging survey among the leading firms shows immediately that the 'traditional' and the 'modern' are the two extremes of style. By taking into account a number of other factors such as price, materials, form, visual appeal, marketing policy, design source, durability and function, it becomes possible to assign a place on the continuum between traditional and modern to any one of these major companies. Taking just seven of the leading manufacturers as representatives of the entire field, it is apparent that Marston & Langinger, Alexander Bartholomew and Amdega all cluster towards the traditional end of the spectrum, while companies like Baco, Halls, Eden and Room 2000 are on the modern end of it. This is not to imply in any way a qualitative judgement – although some would maintain that a manufacturer's style, whether he turns out a traditional or a modern conservatory, does inevitably affect the design characteristics and the level of craftsmanship in the product. This is reflected in a firm's approach to manufacturing, its methods of production, the materials used, the form of the product, the visual appearance, and by no means least it is also reflected in the product price.

One of the main differences in modern design is quite literally a material one between firms producing ranges in aluminium and those who manufacture in wood – normally high quality red cedar imported from Canada, lauan from South America, and Siberian pine. To some extent the choice of material dictates the form of the conservatory, so that aluminium lends itself more readily to smoothly flowing curvilinear forms than does wood. At the same time aluminium imparts an appearance more appropriate to the modern house, while wood seems to harmonise more naturally with older buildings. Manufacturing exclusively in aluminium, companies like Halls, Eden and Crittal Warmlife, by way of example, achieve a visually pleasing range of just such curvilinear designs. Manufacturing only in wood, companies like Marston & Langinger and Bartholomew still incline towards a bespoke service in which traditional conservatories are designed and made to order. By contrast, but still in the field of

This specially designed conservatory forms the main lounge area of Grange Park Hotel in Willerby, near Hull.

Many a public house now has its conservatory where food catering is offered as can be seen from this Amdega special at the Corner House Pub in Newcastle-upon-Tyne.

Standard Amdega conservatories are a popular feature with some new housing developments in Potton.

traditional conservatories, Richardson was known for its original Victorian designs – these have since been inherited by Amdega Limited of Darlington, who in 1971 emerged as the new company when the former W. Richardson & Company was restructured. Shortly afterwards Ken Holliday, then the firm's technical manager (now its technical director) began to consider ways in which Richardson designs might be adapted to batch production and modular assembly without losing any of their quality of craftsmanship. It was an approach worthy of those Victorian innovators, worthy even of approval from Joseph Paxton himself. This particular approach to design and production, supplemented by individually manufactured sections, makes for an exceptionally versatile structure which can be readily adapted to meet almost any requirement. The adoption of Holliday's ideas at Amdega's Faverdale plants in Darlington has helped sweep the company into the position of brand leader in traditional-style conservatories, offering a competitively priced product range in the domestic conservatory market.

In the volume market exactly the opposite has happened – both for aluminium and timber conservatories. Instead of starting with bespoke designs and then developing ways of batch producing them, standard designs were the starting point and then ways were sought of 'tailoring' the better quality ones to meet individual needs.

3
The Buying Routes

Some purchasers of conservatories are certain of the particular model they require and of the dimensions that will satisfy their chosen site, and go ahead confidently purchasing either from a retailer or by forwarding an order direct to a particular manufacturer. The majority, however, are more diffident and prefer to confirm their ideas with an expert. So before making up their mind they arrange a visit from one or more of the various manufacturers' representatives, or from a retailer consultant who can advise on several different makes of conservatory. Some companies demand a fee for this kind of site visit service. Machin Conservatories, by way of example, reputedly ask £50 (1986) for an initial advisory visit. While this practice is understandable because it must discourage time-wasting whimsical enquiries, other suppliers prefer to adopt a policy whereby they make no charge for an initial visit of this kind and so make no attempt to discriminate between the committed and the putative purchaser. For instance, Amdega Conservatories has a number of regional consultants throughout the UK who will arrange to call on potential clients, advise on the feasibility of their initial ideas and be prepared to offer alternative solutions that will go as far as possible towards realising expectations. These consultants will also estimate costs, discuss delivery dates, provide information on planning, building and erection. As part of their comprehensive consultancy service they will draw up site plans, sections and elevations to show how the conservatory will look before the project is taken any further – all free of charge.

Similarly, some retailers – especially nationally operating concerns like Banbury Homes & Gardens – offer a free consultancy service covering conservatories of several different makes. They can tell you how some models can be 'tailored' to individual needs, advise on basework requirements and give you details of their comprehensive service which normally includes erection of the building.

This chapter has been written in two sections. The first details the 'direct from manufacturer' route of buying a conservatory, using Amdega as the example. It does this through an account of a day the author spent in the company of Peter Cawdell, who is Amdega's consultant for a quite extensive region embracing the counties of Cambridgeshire, Bedfordshire, Buckinghamshire and Hertfordshire. It also follows the progress of one particular purchaser who decided to undertake his own building and erection work having purchased a standard Amdega conservatory. This is preceded by information on the company's background, its modern approach to traditional

PREVIOUS PAGE

This attractive lean-to conservatory has one gable and excluded for fitting into the corner of the house exterior.

conservatory design, its designs and methods of operation.

The second part of the chapter covers the 'specialist retailer' route of conservatory buying by detailing the operating methods of Banbury Homes & Gardens Limited. It gives information about the different makes of conservatories available, outlines the company's history and marketing policy, and explains how they set out to simplify the decision making process and turn it into an enjoyable experience.

THE AMDEGA ROUTE

Within the field of traditional conservatory manufacturing Amdega Limited occupies a unique position and operates in remarkable contrast to both Marston & Langinger and Alexander Bartholomew. Amdega was formerly part of W. Richardson Limited, a company which first entered the market in 1874 at the peak of the first great conservatory era. In 1969, however, Amdega became independent of the original Richardson company, although it inherited all its parent's tradition and expertise, in addition to its design portfolio.

W. Richardson was a Darlington-based company; Amdega has remained in Darlington too and the town's Faverdale area is the firm's administrative and production headquarters. While Alexander Bartholomew, Marston & Langinger and others do share the market for traditional conservatories with Amdega, Amdega actually dominates it. The firm's share of the traditional market in 1984 could be put conservatively at 33 per cent, so in this Amdega remains unquestionably the giant. The company readily acknowledges the fact that its long history and vast experience gave it a headstart at the renaissance of the conservatory in the late 1960s and early 1970s. And the firm was well placed to take advantage of this ongoing revival of interest, establishing itself as the undisputed market leader which it still remains. Amdega's success is a tribute to management expertise which has been responsible for technical innovation and energetic marketing. The company's production methods strike the optimum balance between time-honoured craftsmanship and the batch production of modular elements, both of which are subsequently integrated to fulfil any particular order. As the company's technical director explains to visitors, Amdega has modified and adapted original and highly acclaimed Richardson designs – many of them formerly executed in cast iron – without compromising their integrity in any discernible way. Using advanced process technology to produce a range of standard modules enables the company to achieve dramatic cost savings. This makes Amdega products highly competitive, and benefits the customer who gets the equivalent of a custom-built conservatory costing about half the normal price of a

A double lean-to extension provides a large extension to the house.

Computer aided design of Amdega's traditional conservatories.

specially built model. In design the company is no less progressive. In 1984 the firm installed the most advanced computer technology then available to help improve the customised designs of its traditional Victorian conservatories. Amdega was almost certainly the first conservatory company to invest in computer aided design (CAD), and its range of modular components makes the CAD system ideally suited to its draughting requirements. All the details of these modular units are stored in computer memory and are subsequently available when modelling a specific conservatory on screen prior to the production of technical and engineering drawings. Modular units can be incorporated into bespoke designs for individual customers.

Shopfloor capacity at Amdega is truly impressive. In addition to its Neasham Road factory where Richardson conservatories were first manufactured from 1874, the firm has two other plants – one a former locomotive and railway rolling-stock shed, the other a former steel factory: in total it occupies nine acres of Darlington's urban landscape. The dynamics of success in the market place produced spectacular results – for instance, in just one year (1984) the company increased its workforce threefold to reach 150 employees in order to cope with the growing demand for its products from both home and overseas markets.

There is about Amdega conservatories an indefinable quality that results from the interplay between several design factors. The popularity of the product is unquestionably associated with its aesthetic value: the form of each conservatory is visually pleasing in the way it recaptures the elegant style of the Victorian era.

Fig 4–7 (pp 50–3) Plans for a proposed conservatory in Keyworth, Nottingham-shire

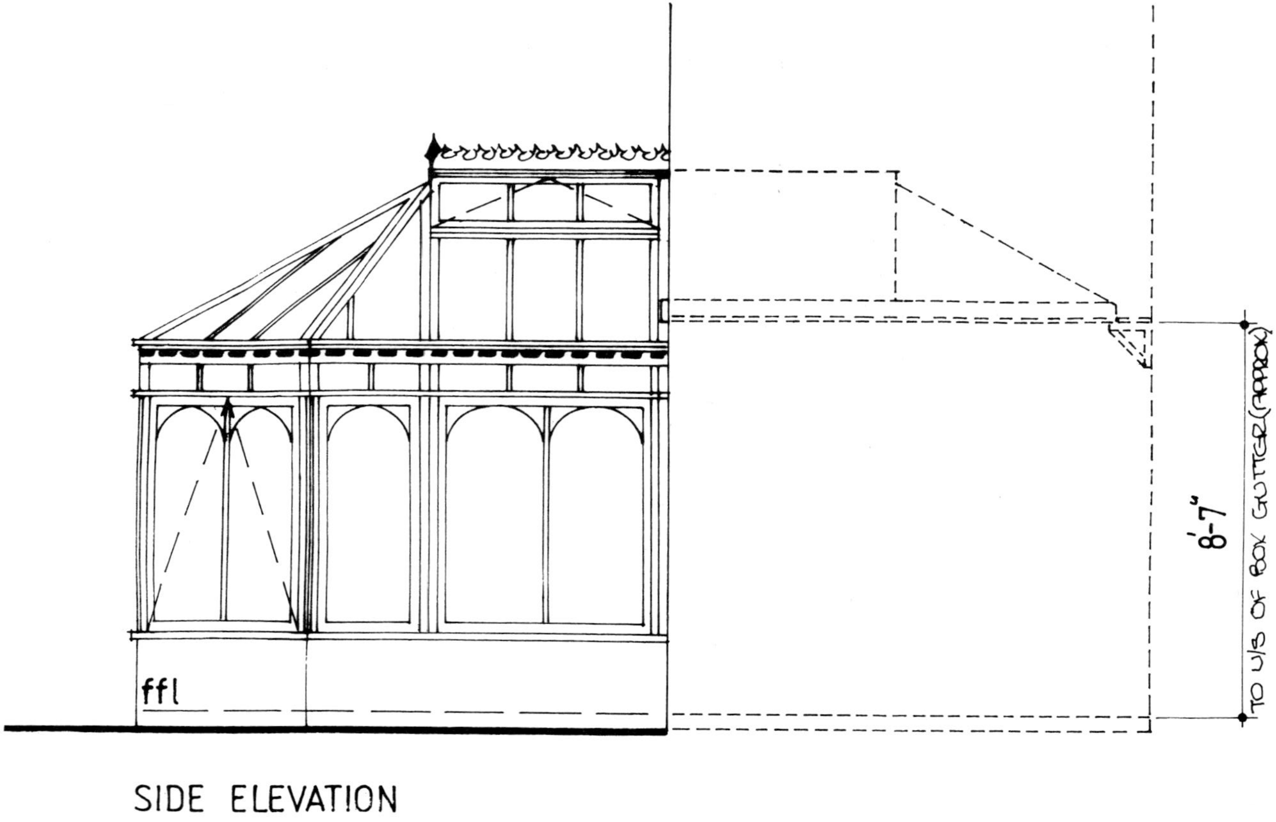

8'-7"

TO U/S OF BOX GUTTER (APPROX)

ffl

SIDE ELEVATION

Fig 4

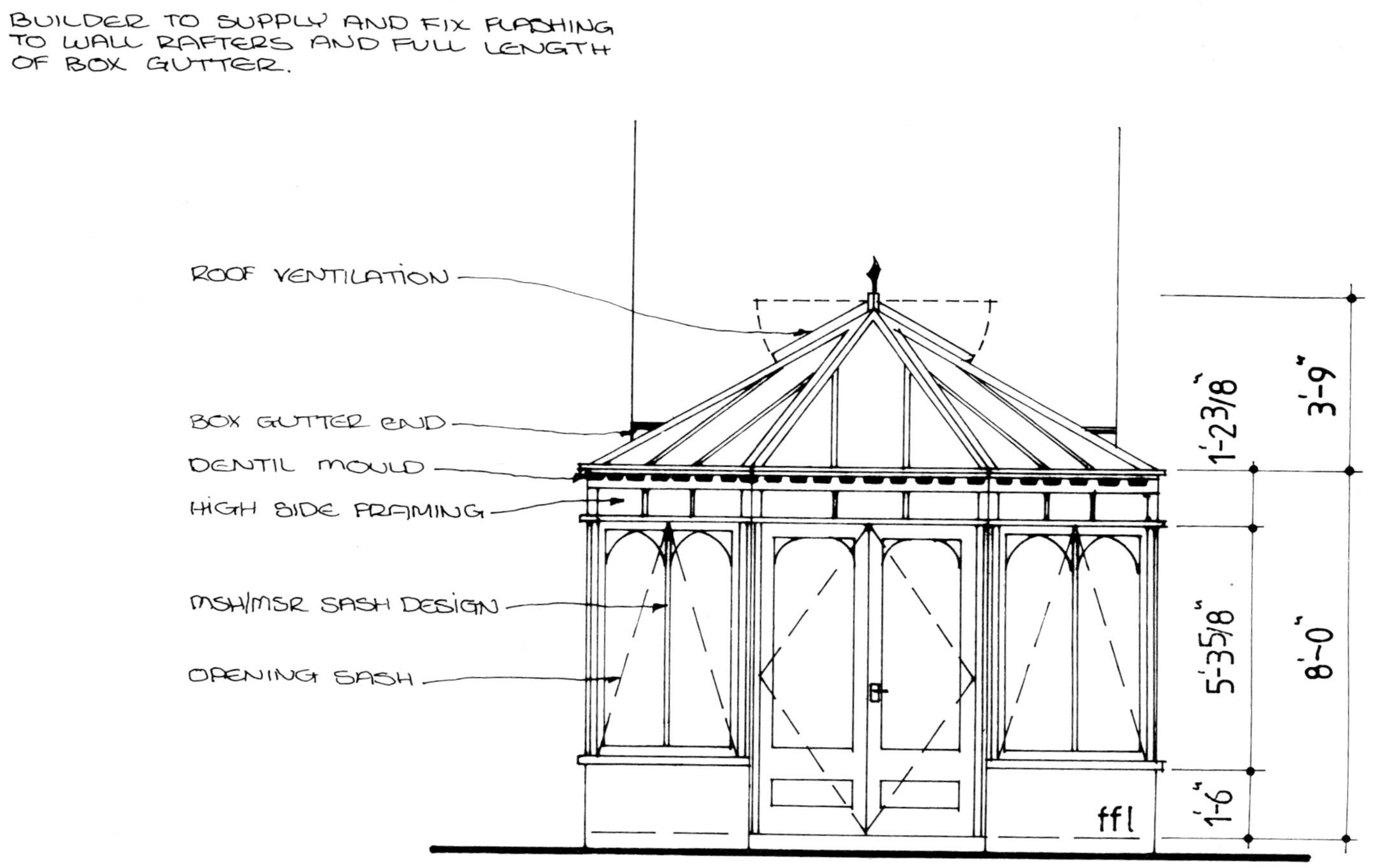

BUILDER TO SUPPLY AND FIX FLASHING
TO WALL RAFTERS AND FULL LENGTH
OF BOX GUTTER.

ROOF VENTILATION

BOX GUTTER END

DENTIL MOULD

HIGH SIDE FRAMING

MSH/MSR SASH DESIGN

OPENING SASH

3'-9"

8'-0"

1'-23/8"

5'-35/8"

1'-6"

ffl

FRONT ELEVATION

Fig 5

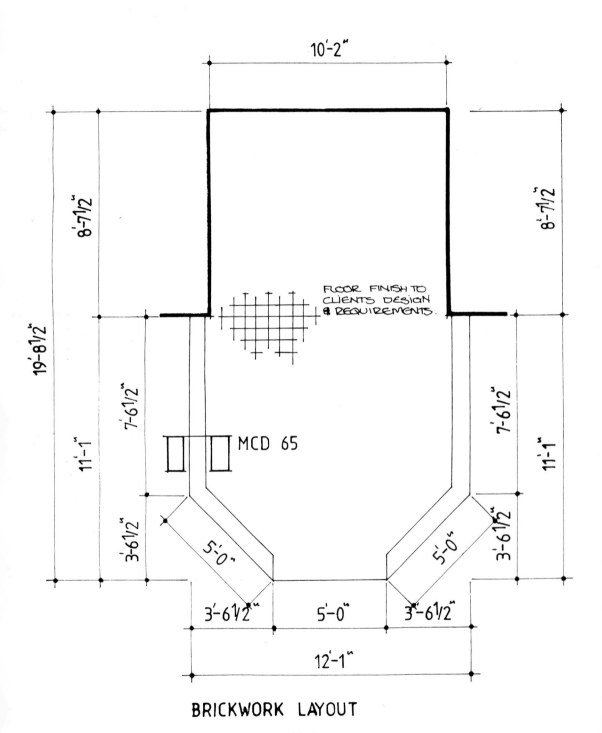

10'-2"

8'-7½"

8'-7½"

19'-8½"

FLOOR FINISH TO
CLIENTS DESIGN
& REQUIREMENTS.

7'-6½"

7'-6½"

11'-1"

11'-1"

MCD 65

3'-6½"

5'-0"

5'-0"

3'-6½"

3'-6½"

5'-0"

3'-6½"

12'-1"

BRICKWORK LAYOUT

Fig 6

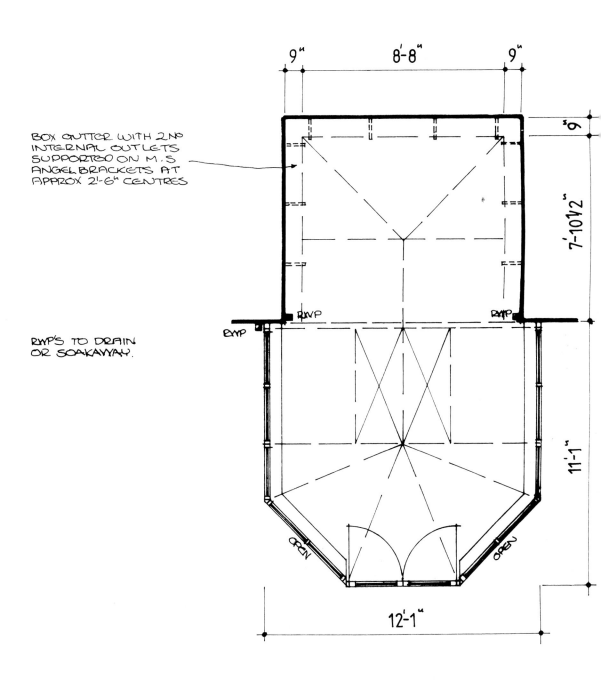

BOX GUTTER WITH 2 NO
INTERNAL OUTLETS
SUPPORTED ON M.S
ANGEL BRACKETS AT
APPROX 2'-6" CENTRES

RWP'S TO DRAIN
OR SOAKAWAY.

9"   8'-8"   9"

9"

7'-10½"

RWP   RWP

RWP

11'-1"

OPEN   OPEN

12'-1"

GENERAL PLAN

Fig 7

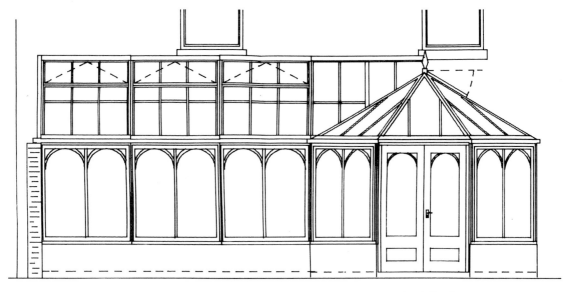

BUILDER TO SUPPLY AND FIX LEAD OR ALUMINIUM FLASHINGS
TO WALL RAFTERS AND LEAN-TO RIDGE AGAINST EXISTING.

BUILD WOODPADS INTO DWARF WALL
FOR FIXING DOOR POSTS.

FRONT ELEVATION

Fig 8

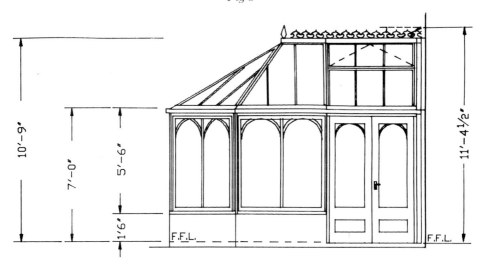

SIDE ELEVATION

Fig 9

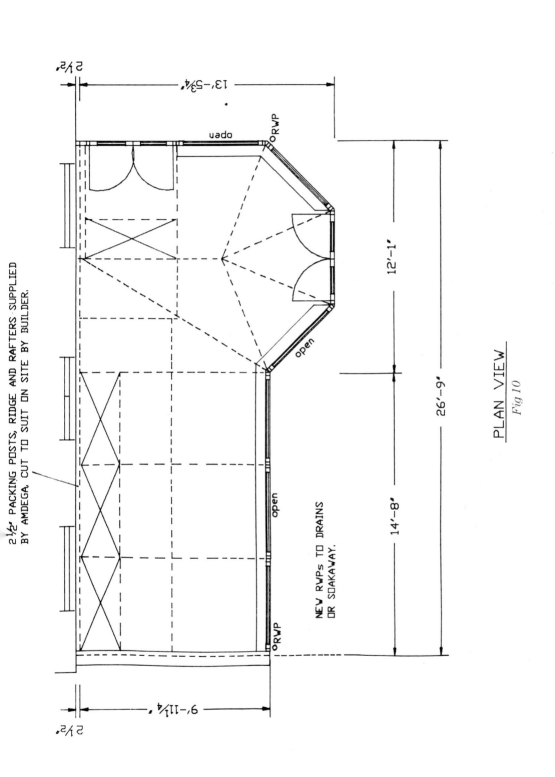

2½" PACKING POSTS, RIDGE AND RAFTERS SUPPLIED BY AMDEGA, CUT TO SUIT ON SITE BY BUILDER.

open

open

open

RWP

RWP

RWP

NEW RWPs TO DRAINS OR SOAKAWAY.

2½"

2½"

13'-5¾"

9'-11¼"

12'-1"

14'-8"

26'-9"

PLAN VIEW

Fig 10

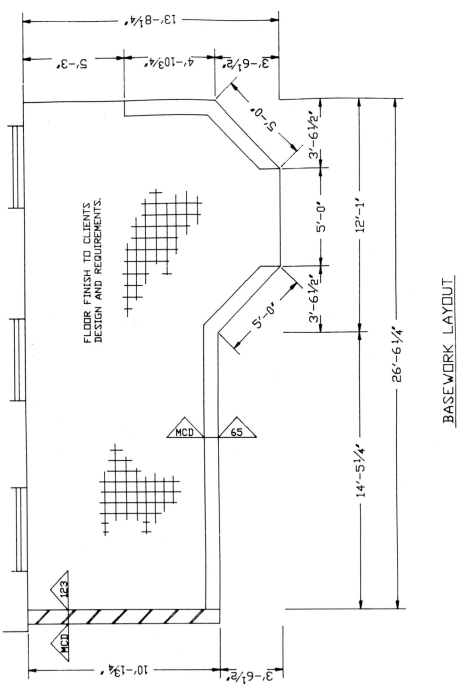

BASEWORK LAYOUT

Fig 11

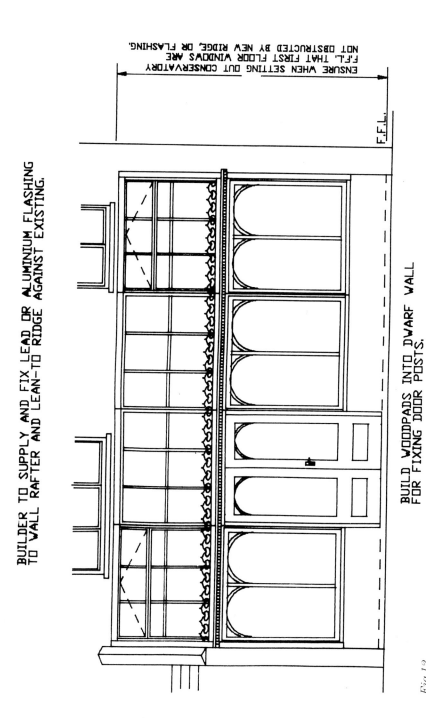

BUILDER TO SUPPLY AND FIX LEAD OR ALUMINIUM FLASHING
TO WALL RAFTER AND LEAN-TO RIDGE AGAINST EXISTING.

ENSURE WHEN SETTING OUT CONSERVATORY
F.F.L. THAT FIRST FLOOR WINDOWS ARE
NOT OBSTRUCTED BY NEW RIDGE, OR FLASHING.

F.F.L.

BUILD WOODPADS INTO DWARF WALL
FOR FIXING DOOR POSTS.

FRONT ELEVATION

Fig 12

Fig 12–15 (pp 57–9) Plans for a proposed conservatory in Harrow, Middlesex

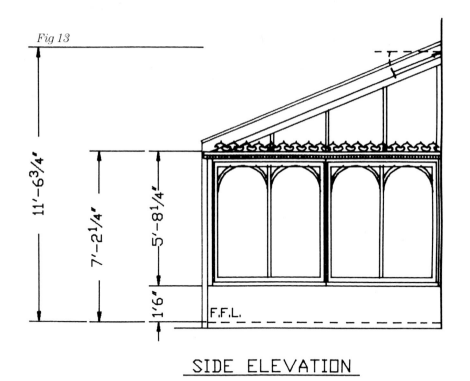

Fig 13

11'-6¾"

7'-2¼"

5'-8¼"

1'6"

F.F.L.

SIDE ELEVATION

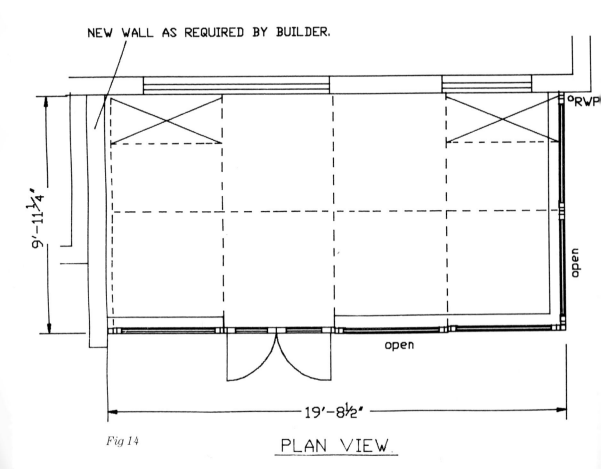

NEW WALL AS REQUIRED BY BUILDER.

RWP

9'-11¼"

open

open

19'-8½"

Fig 14

PLAN VIEW.

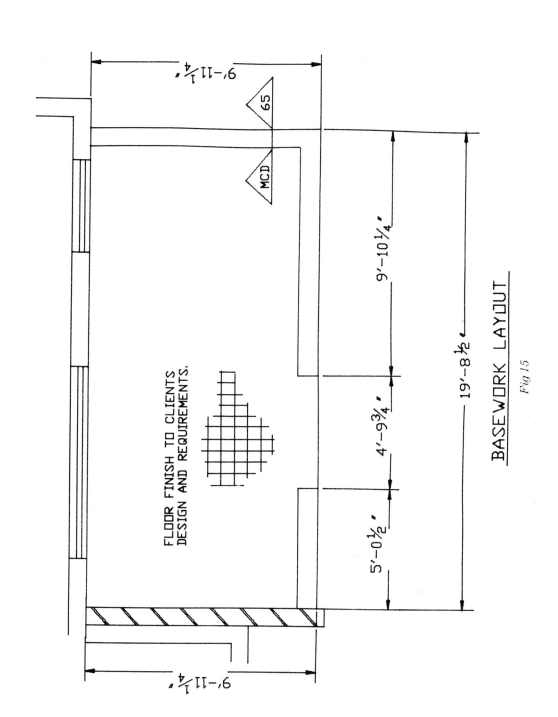

FLOOR FINISH TO CLIENTS
DESIGN AND REQUIREMENTS.

9'-11¼"

65

MCD

9'-10¼"

19'-8½"

4'-9¾"

5'-0½"

9'-11¼"

BASEWORK LAYOUT

Fig 15

This large conservatory not only looks attractive but provides extra living space.

Fig 16–19 (pp 62–4) Plans for a proposed conservatory for a restaurant in Leeds

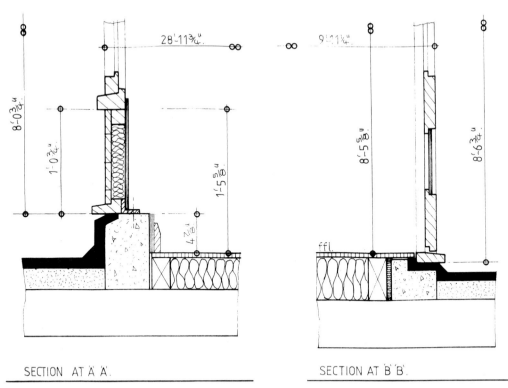

28'-11¾".
9'-11¼".
8'-0¾".
1'-0¾".
1'-5⅝".
4⅞".
8'-5⅝".
8'-6¾".
ffl.
SECTION AT 'A' 'A'.
SECTION AT 'B' 'B'.

Fig 16

BUILDER TO SUPPLY SUITABLE FLASHINGS TO CONS. RIDGE AND END RAFTERS AGAINST EXISTING. ALL AS PER. ARCHITECTS INSTRUCTIONS.
lean to.
oct.
8'-5⅝"
12'-2⅜"
12'-10⅝"
DIMS. TO FFL
SIDE ELEVATION

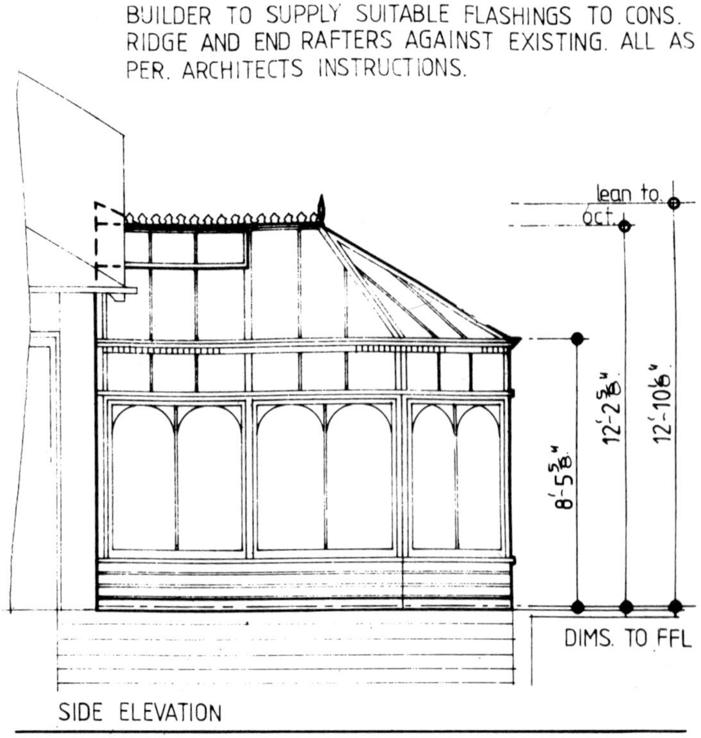

Fig 17

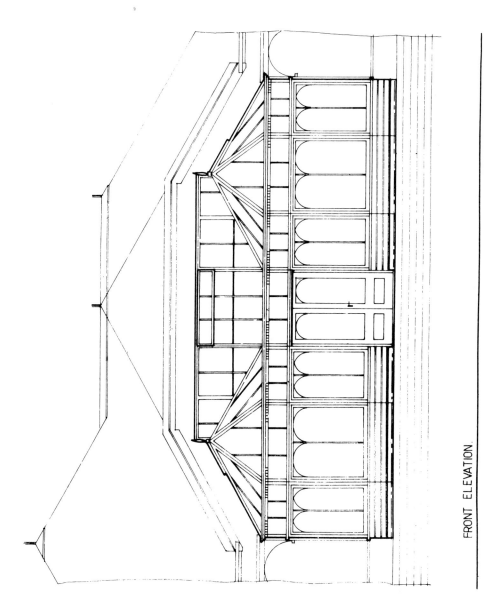

FRONT ELEVATION.

Fig 18

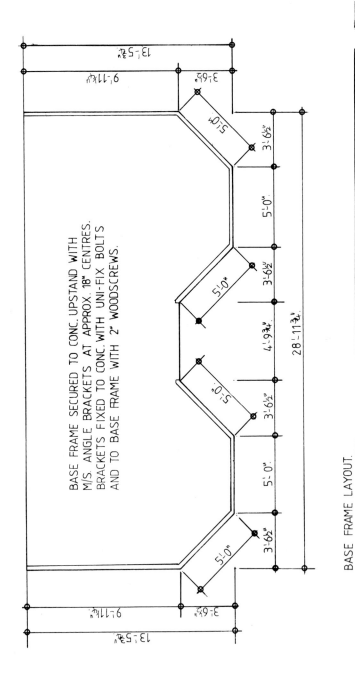

BASE FRAME SECURED TO CONC. UPSTAND WITH M/S. ANGLE BRACKETS AT APPROX. 18" CENTRES. BRACKETS FIXED TO CONC. WITH UNI-FIX BOLTS AND TO BASE FRAME WITH 2" WOODSCREWS.

BASE FRAME LAYOUT.

Fig 19

This new generation of Amdega-designed conservatories is highly functional in the way it can fulfil any one of several different purposes, from enclosing a leisure pool to creating additional living space, as an alternative to providing simply an environment for indoor gardening.

In form and appearance these conservatories harmonise with and complement a wide range of domestic architecture, the effect enhanced by those delightful decorative touches such as dentil moulding around the eaves, and ridge cresting along roof apexes. Materials are also sympathetically chosen – cast iron, long since abandoned as impractical, has given way to wood. Amdega prefers western red cedar, which, although more difficult to work because of its grain, has the advantage of oils that act as a natural preservative and protect it for more than a human lifetime against the elements. Whether treated with cedarwood dressing to leave a natural finish, or white painted, wood is a sympathetic material which blends easily with mature brick or stone-built structures.

A major advantage for customers dealing with large scale operations like Amdega is the much wider range of options available – in other words, greater design choice. For example, there is a choice of five different window sash styles, each of which can radically alter the final appearance of a conservatory. There are two basic types of conservatory, octagonal-ended and lean-to – each is produced in five standard lengths for off-the-peg purchasing, or can form part of a more complex bespoke specification. Single length window glass was recently introduced into all Amdega designs conferring additional benefits of clearer vision, lower energy loss and easier installation. Amdega continues to offer the choice between single and double glazing too. Where heat and sound insulation must be considered, the company offers single glazing where glass roof panels would normally be 0.16in (4mm) thick and larger vertical panels 0.24in (6mm). Naturally, double glazing increases the overall price of a conservatory, but it cuts energy loss by 45 to 50 per cent, reduces sound penetration, and improves levels of security because it is remarkably difficult to penetrate. Homes are generally most vulnerable to burglary at the rear. However, when a double glazed conservatory is added it serves to protect doors and windows which might otherwise be broken or forced open, by enclosing them within a reinforced glass security ring. In view of the fact that double glazing units use toughened glass of the kind fitted into laminated motor-vehicle windscreens, the deterrent effect is perhaps not so difficult to appreciate.

A double lean-to conservatory in the white finish.

OPPOSITE

A single glazed Amdega conservatory used as a summer house and attached to a dwelling in Wisbech, Cambridgeshire.

PAGE 68

Above: *A 12ft × 15ft 10in (3.6 × 4.6m) Amdega model complete with MSH/MSR sashes on a cottage property near Aylesbury, Buckinghamshire.*
Below: *Internal view of an Amdega octagonal/lean-to conservatory tastefully furnished and decorated incorporating MSH/MSR window sashes, dentil moulding and ridge cresting.*

This modular octagonal conservatory is treated with a cedar wood dressing and is a perfect addition to this lovely family house.

A modular design with a special section by Amdega conservatories for a property near Whitchurch.

This double glazed conservatory, which incorporates a link corridor, is complete with extra side framing, dentil moulding and ridge cresting.

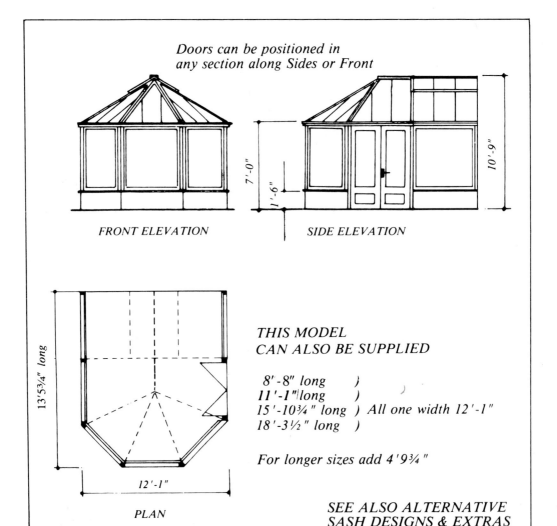

Doors can be positioned in any section along Sides or Front

FRONT ELEVATION   SIDE ELEVATION

7'-0"

1'-6"

10'-9"

13'5¾" long

12'-1"

PLAN

THIS MODEL
CAN ALSO BE SUPPLIED

8'-8" long   )
11'-1" long   )
15'-10¾" long) All one width 12'-1"
18'-3½" long   )

For longer sizes add 4'9¾"

SEE ALSO ALTERNATIVE
SASH DESIGNS & EXTRAS

The above can also be supplied with
1. Box gutter where fitting up to side wall.
2. Gable end for fitting up to Bungalow.
3. With Side Panels removed & brickwork
   up to eaves (party wall).

Fig 20 Standard octagonal conservatory

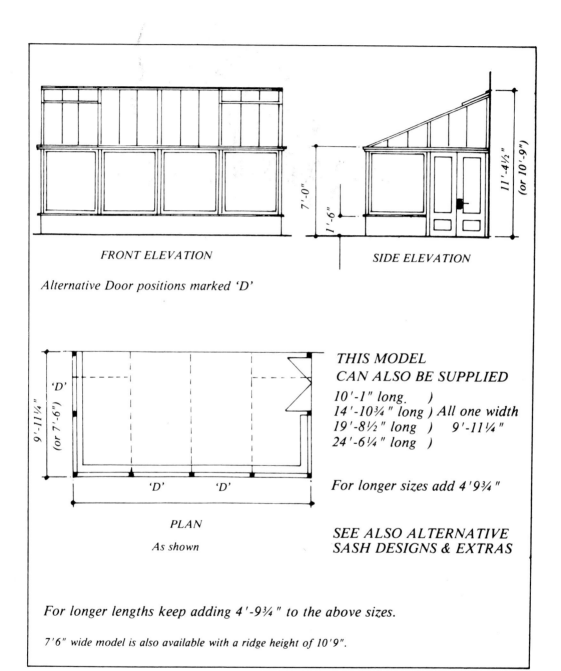

FRONT ELEVATION   SIDE ELEVATION

Alternative Door positions marked 'D'

THIS MODEL
CAN ALSO BE SUPPLIED
10'-1" long.   )
14'-10¾" long) All one width
19'-8½" long   )   9'-11¼"
24'-6¼" long   )

For longer sizes add 4'9¾"

PLAN

As shown

SEE ALSO ALTERNATIVE
SASH DESIGNS & EXTRAS

For longer lengths keep adding 4'-9¾" to the above sizes.

7'6" wide model is also available with a ridge height of 10'9".

Fig 21 Standard lean-to conservatory

SITE VISIT 1

Peter Cawdell's first call of the morning was to a spacious house set in its own extensive, landscaped gardens situated in Georgian Hadley Wood near Barnet – the last suburb on the way out of London to the North. More than 200 years old, this turned out to be a dwelling closely associated with the literary world. To the best of the owners' knowledge Anthony Trollope had once lived there, and more recently, the owners said, Kingsley Amis. At the time this site visit took place the present owners had only been in residence six months and were still very much involved in furnishing rooms and re-arranging interior space to meet their own domestic requirements. One particular problem had been encountered with the split-level kitchen floor, and a number of accidents had occurred when visitors who had failed to notice the change in floor levels lost their balance and took a tumble. Consequently the owners had determined that the first priority was to move the kitchen. A more appropriate domestic space had been earmarked for this with a level floor, but it was not large enough to provide both cooking and dining space. The answer was to extend this particular room. However, choice in the kind of extension that could be added was restricted, firstly because the house was a Grade Two listed building; also because a vociferous local conservation society was lobbying local property owners trying to prick their conscience about preserving the character of their Georgian homes; and by the local authority Planning Department. Taking these factors into account, and on the basis of past experience, the owners had concluded that submission of a plan to add a conservatory to function as a breakfast and morning room was a solution that perhaps all parties would respond to more sym-pathetically. This idea held further advantage because thanks to the house's status as a listed building the project would not be subject to Value Added Tax, thus making a saving of 15 per cent.

Amdega's potential clients discussed their idea with the company's consultant, out of which an outline plan was developed. The solution called for an octagonal conservatory with dimensions of 13ft 5in (4.1m) (projecting out from the proposed cooking area into the garden) by 12ft 1in (3.34m). It was particularly important to the client that the conservatory floor should dispense with a sill and be flush level with the existing domestic floor level. So that the imposing mass of the house itself did not dwarf the conservatory and make it seem insignificant, it was decided the structure should incorporate extra-height side-framing.

Major consideration was given to heating and ventilating this conservatory. Single glazed structures with 0.16in (4mm) thick glass are estimated to have a U value (heat loss measurement) of about

This wall was to be removed and a conservatory added.

two units. By comparison, modern domestic standards of insulation would combine to give a U value of about 0.65 of a unit. The clients specified their conservatory should have no connecting doors to the kitchen area. Again, this would not make for the conservation of heat, so in order to reduce potential heat loss by approximately 40 per cent compared with single glazing it was decided this conservatory should be double glazed. Some form of heating would also be installed sufficient to heat the space, but the domestic central heating – a wet system – would not be extended to the conservatory because it was controlled by an exterior thermostat responding to outside air temperature. The answer would be to install one or more independent units – probably electric. Where ventilation was concerned, there would be side and top opening casements as well as an electric ceiling fan.

If carefully co-ordinated, such a project would take only three weeks to complete following delivery of the conservatory's timber sections. First would come the clearance of the site, the installation of the basework and the building of the dwarf walls. This would be undertaken by the clients' own builder. Amdega's team would then come on site to erect the superstructure. This done, the builder would return to put in the floors, sills and flashings, and the structure would then be painted – Amdega advise a microporous, resin-based paint. The Amdega team would then return to glaze the structure to make it weatherproof and ready for furnishing and occupation.

Client and consultant discuss the removal of a glazed porch and its replacement with an Amdega conservatory.

S*ITE* V*ISIT* 2

The second visit was to a detached Victorian house that was in a state of genteel disrepair, but which possessed considerable character and enjoyed a delightful location. It was full of paintings and sculptures which engendered a congenial atmosphere of creativity and artistic endeavour. The owners were part way through a plan in which they were redesigning their existing garden themselves to provide a croquet lawn, garden pond and a series of descending levels to the rear door of the house, all discreetly screened by mature fruit trees. Part of this plan included the replacement of an existing structure – more a glazed extension on brick walls enclosing the rear door to the garden than a conservatory – which presented a rather sad spectacle and seemed some way past its best.

With only limited space available on this particular site, careful measurements by Amdega's consultant quickly showed that the maximum length of the conservatory could be 11ft 1in (3.34m). It was decided the octagonal form conservatory with ridge cresting and dentil moulding would be most appropriate for the property, as the Victorian style of the timber structure would relate closely to the Victorian architecture of the dwelling. Peter Cawdell recommended the conservatory door be set on the first angle of the octagonal end bay, with a tiled sill (more hard wearing) rather than a timber one. The clients were particularly enthusiastic about having a special kind of glazing that allowed the ultra-violet wavelength in natural sunlight to penetrate. This was not a brand normally fitted by the manufacturer, but Cawdell knew of the product and undertook to discover its availability and whether it could readily be incorporated into the standard structure without extensive modifications that might in turn generate additional costs at the production stage.

The main problem with this scheme proved to be the time factor, since at least three months should be allowed for manufacture, building work and erection. Given ideal weather conditions, once the building work has been completed, an Amdega conservatory's timber superstructure can be erected by an experienced team in three days. It would then take a couple of days to paint, with two additional days to dry and harden; glazing would normally take a further two to three days. Unfortunately the clients in this case especially wanted an Amdega conservatory in time for Christmas, and this was already the end of September. The existing extension would have to be demolished, foundations and dwarf walls put in for the new conservatory, and there was no way of predicting how many days might be lost to bad weather. It was a very tight programme – under the circumstances too tight – and consequently Peter Cawdell declined to guarantee a completion date that would permit furnishing and occupation by 25 December.

The right hand side of this house with its kitchen window and utility room doorway would be enclosed within the conservatory, while a two-storey extension would be built on the left-hand side

S*ITE* V*ISIT* 3

First call of the afternoon was to a late 1920s detached house in Borehamwood, which had been occupied by the same family through three successive generations. The house had been surrounded by open fields until the 1960s when with the arrival of the commuter rail link the area was designated as an overspill town. Thereafter, to the disappointment of the present owners, one development had succeeded another, and their privacy had been progressively eroded. Extended to one side already to provide a utility room with a bedroom above, plans had been passed for a two-storey extension to the rear of the property that would provide further living space downstairs and a master bedroom above with en suite bathroom. Until the early 1980s these particular clients had been agreeably screened by rows of mature trees growing in a larger, detached property on one side with its tennis lawn and well tended gardens. Unhappily for them this neighbouring property was sold and developed to provide low-cost starter home units. The proposed conservatory would help restore some of their lost privacy by incorporating a wall of brickwork to the full height of the eaves that would compensate to some extent for the loss of the intervening trees.

The site chosen for the conservatory was a patio area raised above the level of the garden. With the double-storey extension on one side and a white-painted rough-cast brick wall against the boundary line of the neighbouring property on the other, the conservatory would nestle in an area 20ft (6.09m) wide and 13ft 4in (4.05m) long. It would feature an octagonal end half-module to its corner and would be an integrated octagonal lean-to structure reaching 7ft 6in (2.28m) to the ridge height. This would go some way towards meeting the clients' requirements for a straightforward lean-to design rather than a more 'fancy' one that they felt might be less compatible with what they perceived as the more 'functional' aesthetic of their house. They expressed a concern that anything of a decorative nature might appear to be pretentious. They already knew exactly what purpose their conservatory would fulfil. It would not be for sitting out in; it would serve as a feature to help balance the proportions of the house by retaining its essential symmetry. It would be a garden room with double outward-opening doors, and it would be a space where their three young children would be welcome to indulge in activities of a more 'messy' nature. Above all, the conservatory would be a place for plants – and for the benefit of children and plants alike it would be double glazed to give a higher standard of insulation particularly during the winter months.

$S\underline{ITE}$ $V\underline{ISIT}$ 4

A late eighteenth-century house on Hadley Common rises imposingly from between two cottages to look over the village pond where dragonflies dart with sophisticated acrobatics among the reeds and reproachful moorhens slip across the surface setting up slim bow-waves as they paddle discreetly past. Like the house at Hadley Wood, this too is a house with literary connections. The nineteenth-century writer William Makepeace Thackeray once lived here. Thackeray and Trollope were contemporaries, and living in the same neighbourhood they might have been acquainted. But building a twentieth-century conservatory onto this Hadley Common home produced its own story, posed a dilemma for the owners, and left them to decide how the scenario would finally end.

The owners already had a custom-made leisure lounge on one side of the pleasant courtyard at the rear of their property. This timber-clad structure with its flat roof and metal-framed windows and doors, had been built and erected by a local carpenter twenty-three years previously. It was redolent of the designs and architecture of that era, and seemed to have borrowed something both from the utility style of the war years, and also – while still making loyal references to the Bauhaus principles of functionalism governing form – from that debased international style that was becoming more prevalent in those discredited mass housing projects of the 1960s. Even if this geometrically harsh timber structure made no concessions to decorative features it remained, nonetheless, a remarkable tribute to the qualities of workmanship and materials that had originally gone into its construction. It was only now, almost a quarter century later, that the fabric of its roof had finally surrendered to the English weather. Unfortunately it made an incongruous addition anyway, as its style was completely antithetical to the architecture of this 200-year-old property. The intention was to replace this weathered leisure lounge with an Amdega conservatory. There were, however, a number of site factors that had to be considered carefully first, which was why the company's regional consultant had been asked to call.

The existing timber structure had been erected in a position which although sheltered, did not get the sun at all because of a high wall. The opposite side of the courtyard, by comparison, was a suntrap, enjoying a substantial amount of sunshine. Erecting a conservatory on the same site as the existing lounge would deprive it of sunlight

OPPOSITE

A timber clad leisure lounge is the proposed site for an Amdega conservatory.

and thereby make it a less inviting environment – at least that was the potential danger. Nor would there be direct access from the dwelling into the conservatory, so it would probably be less used in bad weather. The owners, however, had considered these two major points. They had recognised that the old leisure lounge was neither attractive nor sympathetic and had concluded that an Amdega conservatory would be more so. They also accepted the conservatory would have very little sun and was unlikely to be much used outside the summer months. Consequently their aim was to purchase a single glazed octagonal form that would be approximately 12ft (3.64m) long and 13ft 2in (3.9in) wide.

One of the advantages of having an Amdega consultant make an initial site visit is that ideas may be confirmed, or alternative propositions put forward for consideration. In this case there certainly was an alternative solution. It would prove more costly, but the benefits would be twofold. The ageing leisure lounge would still be demolished, but the site on the other side of the courtyard would be used. Located here the conservatory would enjoy sunlight throughout the year, and with direct access from within the house instead of having to walk across an open courtyard, it was more likely to be used all the year round. The conservatory could be positioned between the gable end of the house and the ornamental fish pond, from where it afforded views down the garden to the small gazebo and the swimming pool at the far end. However, this plan brought with it two drawbacks. An area previously dedicated to a sun-lounger settee and plants would have to be given up; there were reservations about integrating the house with the conservatory, and significant differences in level between the courtyard and the house floor would have to be overcome. This would necessitate the building of support brickwork walls and putting in a suspended floor to the conservatory – an external spiral staircase or steps would lead out of it to the garden.

It was a matter that could not be resolved at a stroke, so, having taken a comprehensive series of measurements, Peter Cawdell left this particular site, but not without undertaking to provide plans for both schemes so that they might be examined more fully before a decision was made.

SITE VISIT 5

Final call of the day was to an impressive detached property in Essenden, Hertfordshire; this had formerly been a rectory, built in about 1730, with additions and extensions made to it for over more than a century afterwards, so that its north-west wing dated from the earlier part of the eighteenth century, and its south-east wing from the later nineteenth. It was a dwelling of unique character and had been occupied by its present owners for eight years. Interestingly, the original rectory had been a timber-frame dwelling with a brick infill and rendered external wall. The original oak posts and beams were still in place and would pose some interesting problems when the proposed conservatory was built.

The house was sited on a knoll of land; it had several natural springs close by, and had been surrounded by a shallow and narrow 'moat' to protect it from flooding. The 'moat' was still there, serving as a kind of external damp-proof course that led rain or spring water away from the walls, and would have to be bridged to permit erection of the conservatory. Below the gable end there was a terrace supported by a retaining wall giving way to a lawned area below. Giving way was literally correct. The retaining wall was in the process of slow but inexorable collapse and in time much of the terrace would subside into the garden. On this side of the house were the kitchen and living-room areas. Additional living space was probably the last reason the owners would give for building a conservatory; their intention was to link these two interior domestic areas together through an exterior conservatory, taking the opportunity to clear and rebuild the collapsing terrace at the same time.

The oldest side of the house was the site chosen for the addition of the conservatory, and the site itself was quite extensive – certainly enclosing more than 323sq ft (30sq m). In addition the house was a Grade Two listed building. Consequently because the site was above the 323sq ft (30sq m) limit below which building and planning regulations do not apply, and the house being listed, erecting a conservatory was going to require consent from the Building and Planning Departments of the local authority, as well as approval from the agency for historic buildings. A pair of patio doors opened onto a flight of stone-flagged steps bridging the 'moat' and leading down to the crumbling terrace below; the top of these steps was level with the floor of the house and this would have to be the level of the conservatory floor. It was going to require a considerable amount of brickwork that would then have to be rendered to match the house. As this was a four-storey house of very generous proportions the feeling was that unless the Amdega conservatory were to be equally generous in its proportions it might come to signify little more than a glazed blister. The solution advanced by Amdega's consultant called

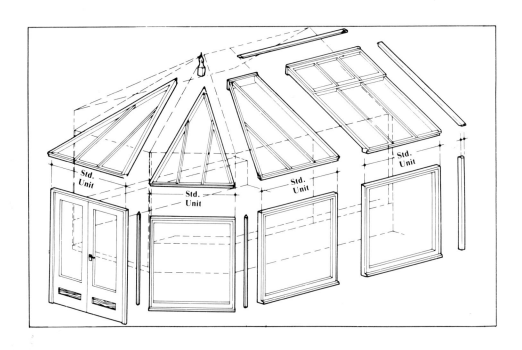

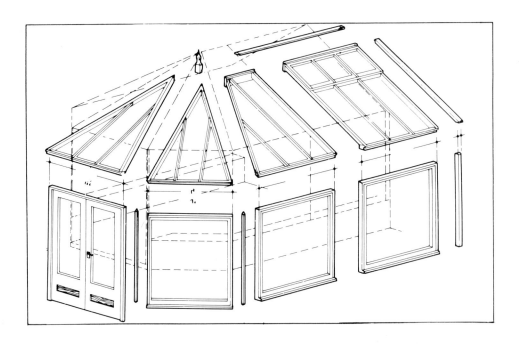

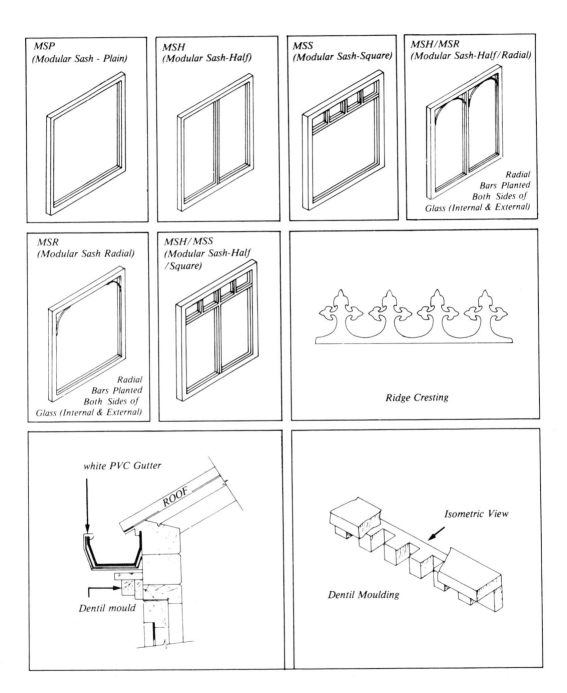

MSP
(Modular Sash - Plain)

MSH
(Modular Sash-Half)

MSS
(Modular Sash-Square)

MSH/MSR
(Modular Sash-Half/Radial)

Radial
Bars Planted
Both Sides of
Glass (Internal & External)

MSR
(Modular Sash Radial)

Radial
Bars Planted
Both Sides of
Glass (Internal & External)

MSH/MSS
(Modular Sash-Half
/Square)

Ridge Cresting

white PVC Gutter

ROOF

Dentil mould

Isometric View

Dentil Moulding

Figs 22 & 23 Amdega offers optional extras and a range of six alternative window sash designs

The site for a very substantial double octagonal conservatory with intervening lean-to section. The conservatory floor will be at about the same level where client and consultant are standing.

for two octagonal modules, each 13ft 9in (4.18m), linked together by means of a lean-to section that would itself be almost 12ft (3.64m) wide. The cost for the entire project was estimated at £30,000 (1986).

So that it would relate to its host structure and the surrounding environment, the conservatory would be double octagonal ended – an Amdega P1 design – and so as to keep the height of the conservatory in scale with the height of the house it was decided that 18in (45.6m) high side-framing would be needed. The clients specified MSH/MSR style window frames, ridge cresting and dentil moulding, and as they intended to use their conservatory throughout the year they required double glazing to be fitted. Gas-fired central heating would also be installed, and it was decided not to extend the existing domestic system, but to fit instead a subsidiary boiler alongside the main heating unit; thus the conservatory could use its own independent system when required without heating the entire house unnecessarily. It was also planned to lay a floor of marble tile, and when completed the structure would be fronted by a terrace wide enough for sitting out and with steps descending to the garden.

The structure would function as a fully glazed verandah – a route carrying domestic traffic between living room and kitchen; as an elegant space for entertaining and relaxing; as a bridge between house and grounds that would ultimately be fitted out with furniture appropriate to both home and garden environments.

SHEILA AND DAVID

For twenty-five years, since first moving into their cottage on the fringe of a small, serene Bedfordshire village very close to the Northamptonshire border, Sheila and David had wanted a greenhouse because they had always been keen gardeners. Neither could raise any real enthusiasm for a conventional, popular, aluminium structure however, because both felt this would detract from the visual unity of their sensitively renovated property. Faced with this problem, their unusual solution was to purchase a conservatory for use exclusively as a greenhouse – at probably six times the cost per square foot. Having taken quite some time to consider which style would most closely match their Restoration cottage, they eventually decided on an octagonal design from Amdega: this they thought would best suit their aesthetic and functional requirements, and also fall within the limits of their budget. Having settled on their choice of manufacturer the question was where best to site the structure.

Now it so happened that back in the early 1960s when David and Sheila had moved into their cottage, there had been a tumbledown outhouse standing on a small patch of ground perhaps twenty or thirty feet from their back door.

'It turned out to have been a shoemaker's tiny workshop,' said David. 'We discovered lasts, bradawls, a range of shoemaking paraphernalia, and strip after strip of leather.' There must have been a genuine cottage industry at one time on the site; however, because Northampton itself – along with urban areas like Higham Ferrers, and Rushden – is noted for its leather goods and footwear manufacturing, perhaps it should come as no great surprise to find a shoemaker's workshop in one of the nearby villages.

'But,' remarked David, 'this handy workspace was in a very dilapidated state when Sheila and I first came here. We believe the original structure could well date from the late seventeenth century – the era of William and Mary between 1689 and 1702. It had been a single-leaf construction with no solid foundations, no damp proofing, no waterproofing under the roof either. Nothing like that. It was in a truly neglected state where you felt a small puff of wind could've demolished it.'

Both David and his wife greatly admire the vernacular architecture that prevailed in rural north Northamptonshire and which is still well in evidence today. The style derives from a distinctive way of building in stone and particularly where it is used with decorative features in the construction of chimneys. As David is himself a highly skilled craftsman, making small pieces of scientific apparatus, like the shoemaker he too needed an industrial workshop of his own. What could be more appropriate than to reconstruct this former shoemaker's workplace and adapt it to his own use?

The former shoemaker's workshop, site for an Amdega octagonal conservatory.

'We decided to dismantle the entire structure and rebuild it to modern standards. But we were absolutely determined to preserve its original appearance,' said David. 'Altogether it took Sheila and I about eighteen months to complete the project. Now I've got a workshop on a concrete base, with cavity walls and a damp course. We laid on mains power and water, and there's solid fuel heating, too.'

'So, the best site as far as we were concerned,' said Sheila, taking up the story, 'had to be adjacent to the south gable end of David's workshop. I'm very keen on horticulture; David prefers growing vegetables. And what we both wanted was a cool greenhouse where we could bring on plants early for planting out. We reckoned we'd three positive factors in favour of this site for our conservatory/ greenhouse. Firstly it provides a south-facing aspect, so there'd be the full advantage of any sunlight and heat; secondly there'd be a fair measure of brickwork and hence less surface area of glass for heat loss. And thirdly there'd be the benefit of a *warm* brick wall in David's workshop – the south wall is the one with the chimney and fireplace in it. That's why we thought single glazing would be ample, and also decided we wouldn't need a heat source in the greenhouse because we want to maintain it as a cool growing environment.'

They eventually selected an octagonal-form conservatory to use as their greenhouse, in natural cedar finish so it would sympathise with the existing workshop structure. At this point the majority of purchasers would have been content to place their order – probably contracting with a local builder to put in foundations and erect the support walls – before allowing an experienced team to come and put up their conservatory. However, David and his wife are exceptional: they decided they would undertake the entire project themselves, and with hard-won building skills gained from refurbishing their cottage and the workshop they were obviously knowledgeable and confident enough to take it on successfully. Just a few months on from their initial decision, the conservatory was complete. With its essential decorative features like radial glazing bars to its window frames, dentil moulding round the eaves, ridge cresting and a finial, it is only the angle of pitch to the greenhouse roof that fails to relate completely to its host building: otherwise the two structures integrate so well it seems as though they might have stood together some considerable time. A single entrance on its west elevation permits gardening activities to proceed with equal facility on both sides. The inner leaf of the dwarf wall supports plant shelving, while the rear brick retaining wall has work-height benching for potting up and other jobs, with removable horizontal members so that plants can grow up unimpeded from the beds beneath. There is no concrete raft by way of foundation here. The intention is to make use of the rich,

The conservatory arrives – sections are stacked in the garage.

friable soil inside the structure to allow natural soakaway drainage, and to provide just a shallow layer of pea gravel dressing as part of the growing medium. So instead of a solid concrete base there are just footings sunk 3ft (0.9m) down on a 9in (22.8cm) concrete platform for the dwarf walls, with an insulating air cavity between and a damp course on the outer leaf only.

'We firmly believe the design fully meets our needs and provides a good many possibilities for serious, amateur gardeners like ourselves to explore,' declared David in reviewing the project. 'As far as the manufacturer's plans are concerned,' he continued in answer to the question, 'yes, we did encounter some small points of difficulty. We didn't realise, for example, that the window sashes came out of their frames. We did notice the drill holes in the sides of the frames, of course, but the instructions didn't actually specify which screws should go where, so it took us a bit of time to sort that one out. Generally, though, if you're erecting the conservatory yourself you'll find Amdega's drawings are quite good and they're easy enough to read once you've got used to them. The only thing we found a bit irritating at first was the way the firm tried to supply a set of common instructions that would cater for all its design variations. Consequently we had to be very careful that we had selected the sections specifically relevant to ourselves. Even so, it didn't take more than four weeks from the delivery of the timberwork to complete the project. Admittedly that was with both of us working on it . . . but only evenings and weekends.'

Major problems? There were none. Sheila and David reported only a couple of minor delays – and one amusing incident when David discovered their cottage's mains water supply with his own pick-head dowsing technique. A mild panic ensued while the stop-tap was located and the supply turned off – but he went on to take advantage of his freshly discovered talents for water-divining by teeing into the main and running in an alkathene branch supply for the greenhouse.

Finding a source of bricks that would match the original sort was not altogether easy. Even a renowned architectural salvage specialist like Prigmores, based not far away and also in Bedfordshire, could not help on this occasion. Prigmores, typical of the resourceful few who recycle buildings and well known to the conserving cognoscenti, can readily supply anything from a terracotta chimney pot at £8 (1986) to a pulpit in oak worth £8,000 (1986) rescued from a church before it was demolished. The yards of these firms are an absolute treasure trove of items, and the work of Prigmores and others is worthy of

OPPOSITE

Dwarf walls are raised.

The Amdega conservatory is almost complete in just four weeks.

some kind of heritage award in acknowledgement of their contribution to vernacular preservation. In the search for bricks, however, David had to cast further afield. But patience and perseverance were eventually rewarded when a supplier was found who could provide not only straight bricks, but inner and outer squint bricks into the bargain. Their only other delay of any consequence was caused by the lack of a scribe section to pack against the doorframe. Fortunately David possessed both the carpentry expertise and the appropriate woodworking machinery to be able to produce the necessary length of A-form section so the brickwork could proceed.

Other than these relatively small instances the entire project went ahead according to schedule. Having completed this greenhouse/conservatory, David jokingly remarked that of course, when he and Sheila get around to putting up the next one they should be able to manage it in less than half the time!

OPPOSITE

David applies beads of sealant to the roof sections ready for glazing.

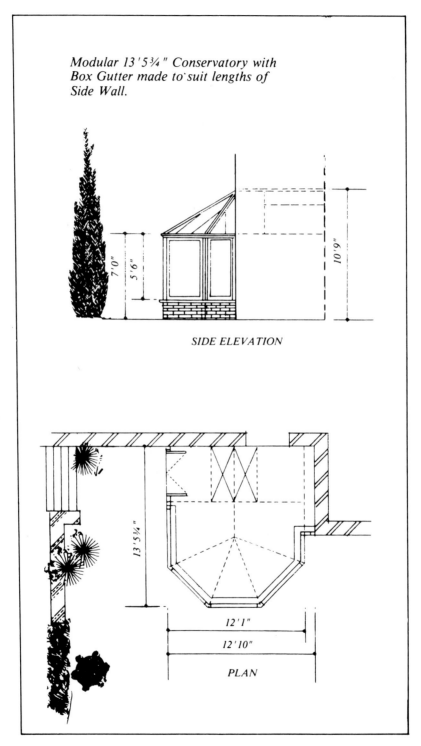

Modular 13'5¾" Conservatory with Box Gutter made to suit lengths of Side Wall.

SIDE ELEVATION

PLAN

Figs 24–33 (pp 94–103) Amdega's modular and special units combine to offer a very wide range of alternatives

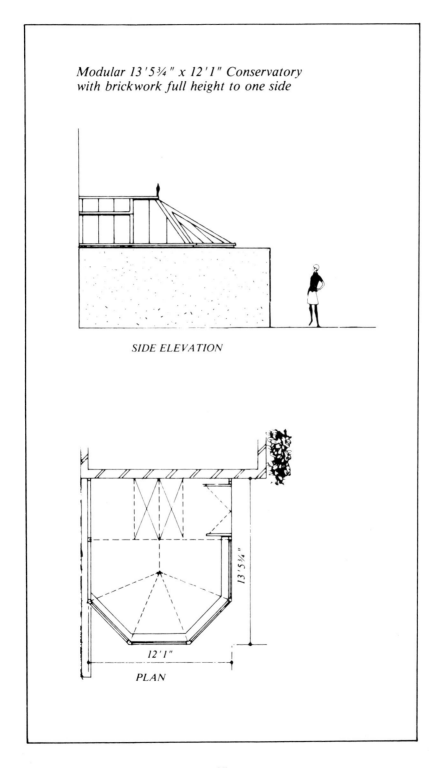

Modular 13'5¾" x 12'1" Conservatory
with brickwork full height to one side

SIDE ELEVATION

PLAN

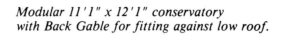

*Modular 11'1" x 12'1" conservatory
with Back Gable for fitting against low roof.*

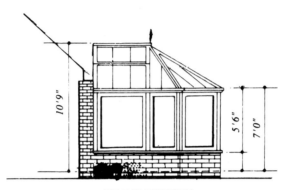

SIDE ELEVATION

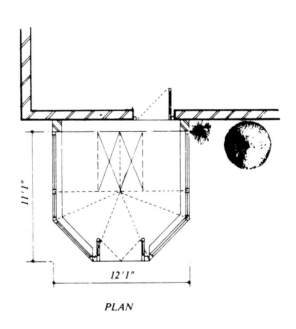

PLAN

Modular/special 13'5¾" x 12'1" Conservatory
Complete with a 2 Bay 9'11¼" wide
Standard lean-to and Valley.

FRONT ELEVATION

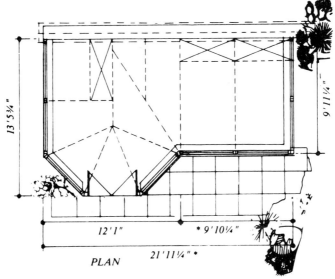

PLAN

* To vary this length add
or subtract 4'9¾"

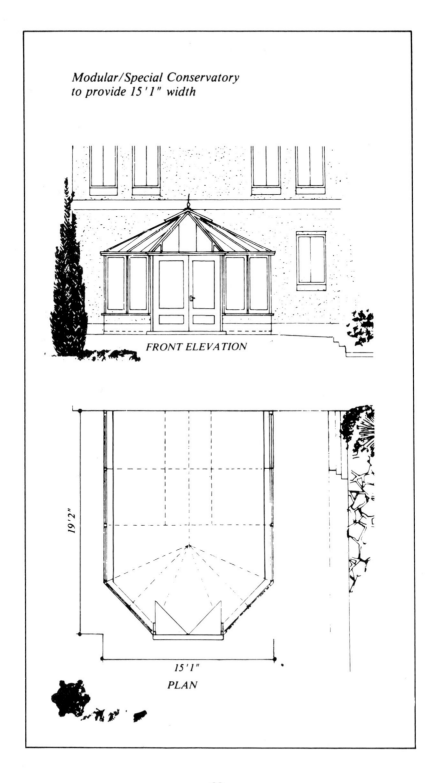

Modular/Special Conservatory
to provide 15'1" width

FRONT ELEVATION

19'2"

15'1"

PLAN

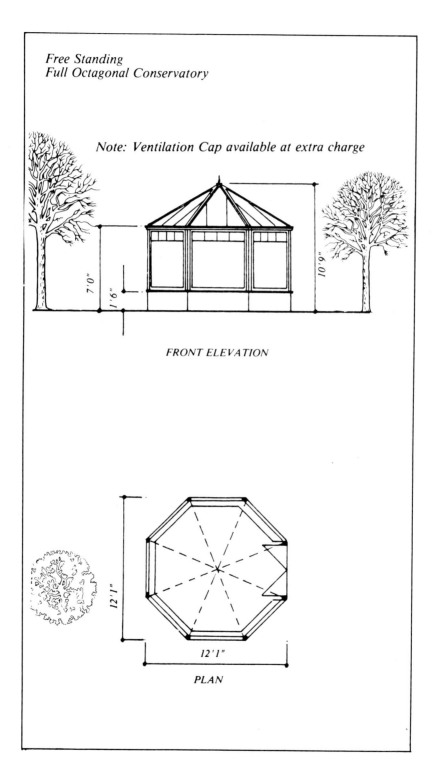

Free Standing
Full Octagonal Conservatory

Note: Ventilation Cap available at extra charge

FRONT ELEVATION

PLAN

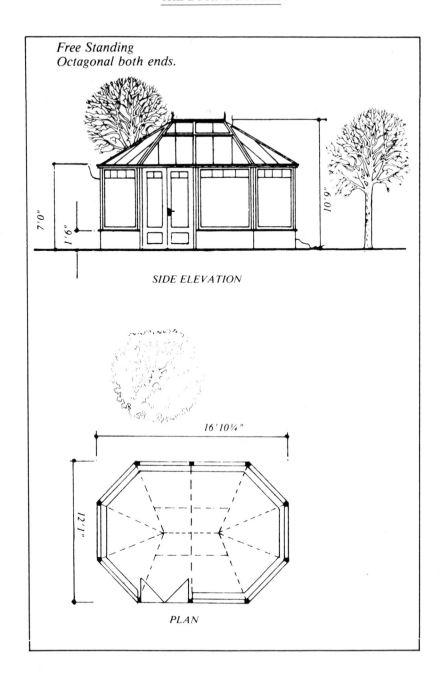

Free Standing
Octagonal both ends.

7'0"

1'6"

10'9"

SIDE ELEVATION

16'10¾"

12'1"

PLAN

OPPOSITE

A single glazed octagonal conservatory by Amdega featuring central heating, rush matting over Welsh quarry tile floor and cane seating from Mentmore & Towers. Attached to a Victorian cottage property situated in the Chiltern Hills.

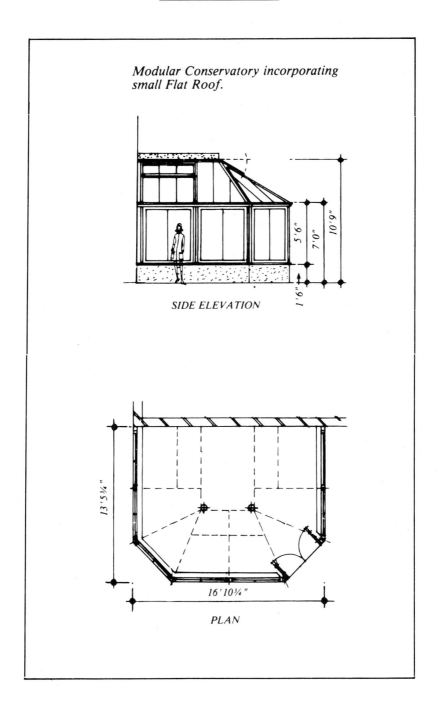

Modular Conservatory incorporating small Flat Roof.

SIDE ELEVATION

PLAN

OPPOSITE

A lean-to conservatory designed and erected by Marston & Langinger for a house near Kew Gardens, London.

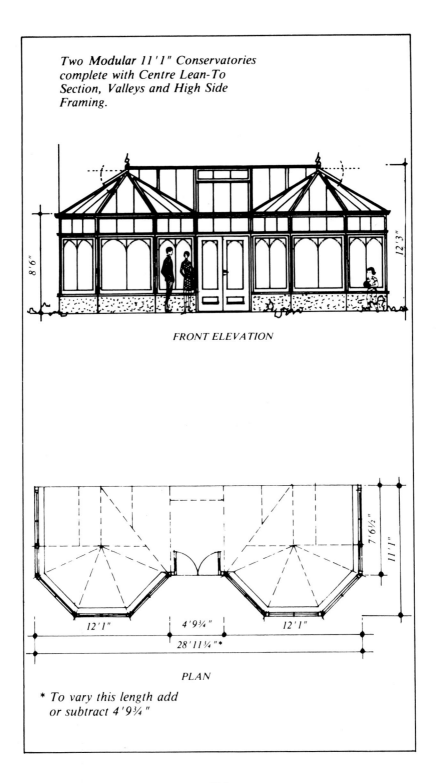

Two Modular 11'1" Conservatories complete with Centre Lean-To Section, Valleys and High Side Framing.

FRONT ELEVATION

PLAN

* To vary this length add
  or subtract 4'9¾"

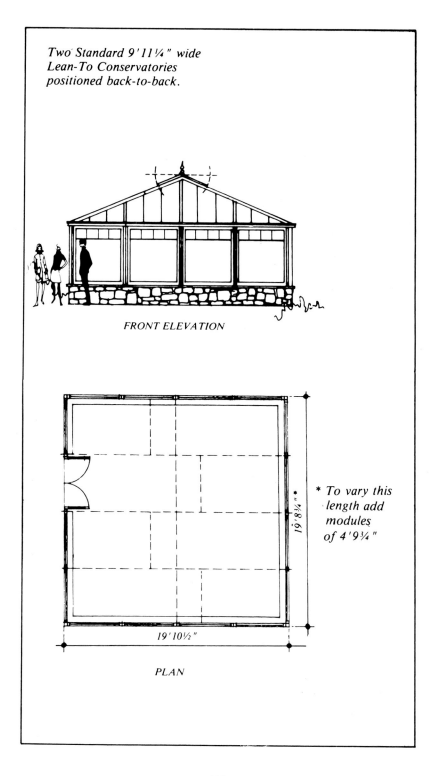

Two Standard 9'11¼" wide
Lean-To Conservatories
positioned back-to-back.

FRONT ELEVATION

* To vary this
length add
modules
of 4'9¾"

19'8¾" *

19'10½"

PLAN

A combination of two back-to-back lean-to roofs. This is a modular special conservatory, finished in natural wood.

THE BANBURY ROUTE

The company now known as Banbury Homes & Gardens Limited started life in 1954 as a producer of concrete garages. Demand for these, plus diversification into other product areas, saw the company grow rapidly. Along the way it acquired a string of others, the most notable of which was Alton, the country's leading producer of cedar greenhouses.

By the late 1950s Banbury was producing a range of conservatories with cedar framework and concrete base walls, and marketing them through its own direct sales organisation. It soon became one of the country's major producers in a market that, from the early 1960s, began to emerge from depression.

The recessionary years of the late 1970s – far from condemning the conservatory to its second period of decline – actually increased its popularity. These were years of financial instability that made people reluctant to take on the additional financial burden that went with moving to a bigger house. Extending their existing dwelling using a conservatory was the lower cost and more convenient.

Alongside this, technological development was turning conservatories into very versatile buildings indeed. Double glazing was no longer the sole province of the bespoke conservatory – it was being introduced into volume production as well; and aluminium was becoming more acceptable as a frame material as durable maintenance-free finishes like polyester powder coating were introduced in a range of attractive colours. This, in turn, led to aluminium greenhouse manufacturers like Baco and Eden turning their attentions to what was beginning to develop into a lucrative conservatory market.

All these factors led to Banbury deciding on a change of direction in the late seventies. Until that time it had sold a limited range of conservatories of its own manufacture and could see that, to be the dominant force in the volume market, it must offer a much wider range, including aluminium models. Banbury already had expertise in producing cedar conservatories and marketing them through its own network of Display Centres and through its nationwide team of Home Advisors. What it DIDN'T have was expertise in designing and manufacturing aluminium conservatories. On the other hand, the leading aluminium conservatory companies were manufacturing companies only, selling their buildings through agents such as garden centres. Banbury recognised that they and existing aluminium conservatory manufacturers had a lot to offer one another.

Thus it was that, as the turn of the decade approached, Banbury started to change its emphasis from being a manufacturing company selling just its own range of conservatories, to being a marketing company selling the best conservatories from several different manufacturers. It set out to be the pace setter in the volume conservatory industry, offering not only the widest range of products available from a single source, but also providing the best display facilities, the best standards of guidance and advice, and a comprehensive back-up service including erection of the building.

The eighties are seeing a continuance and development of this philosophy, with Banbury Display Centres gradually moving towards a still more sophisticated approach. The comfort and convenience of the customer are regarded as all-important; great emphasis is being placed on attractive site layout and comfortable sitting areas where customers can browse through brochures, seek expert advice or discuss financial details in complete privacy.

Buying a conservatory from Banbury normally starts with sending for their comprehensive full colour brochure. This includes a vast range of buildings from a variety of manufacturers and in a choice of materials and in styles ranging from Victorian to ultra-modern, conservatories for occasional use and for full use all-year-round, models for building into or around corners, and others that can be 'tailored' to your needs by providing a virtually limitless range of layout options.

Next you have a choice. You can either ask a Banbury Home Advisor to visit you (without any obligation on your part) to discuss your requirements and advise you, or you can visit one of the company's fifty plus nationwide network of Display Centres. Most people choose the latter alternative, feeling that seeing the buildings on display together is the only way to make realistic comparisons. At the Display Centre you can talk to one of Banbury's Advisors about your requirements safe in the knowledge that the buildings on offer have been selected as being the best available from leading manufacturers and that, because Banbury are free agents, they don't have a vested interest in selling you a building from any one particular manufacturer's range. Because Banbury's Advisor has an intimate knowledge of the buildings and how they can often be tailored to individual needs, he may be able to put forward a variety of options for your consideration. He will be able to show you samples of the different colours that are available, tell you about basework requirements and put you in touch with a builder experienced in this type of work. Alternatively, if you want to save money by undertaking your own basework, he can arrange for you to receive the necessary plans. He can give you an accurate price quote for supplying any of the buildings in the range and erecting it on your ready-prepared base; and he can advise on the various ways of financing the purchase – extending your mortgage or taking out a Home Improvement Loan, for example.

On the strength of your visit to the Display Centre, you may feel you are able to order a conservatory that will suit your needs and the looks of your home, or you may prefer the Banbury Advisor to visit your home, see the situation himself, and give you further advice – entirely without cost or obligation on your part. There's no need to order until you're absolutely sure you've selected a building that's exactly right for your needs.

Once you order, Banbury notify you of delivery and installation dates that take into account your own base laying programme. On conservatories that allow you certain 'tailor-made' options like specifying sliding patio and/or hinged doors, door and window positions and the like, there will be a delay of a few weeks whilst the conservatory is individually made to your requirements at the factory.

Then Banbury's installation team erect the conservatory on your base. They are skilled craftsmen working exclusively for Banbury and are trained to go about their work with the minimum of disruption to your routine. Normally the job takes no more than two days and the installation team will leave the site in a tidy condition once the job is complete.

The range of buildings available from Banbury is constantly reviewed and updated to ensure that it includes the very best conservatories of all types. As we go to press the range includes conservatories by Banbury, Baco, Eden, Hallmark, Halls and Room 2000. A selection of them are described in the remaining pages of this chapter.

THE BANBURY SOVEREIGN AND SOVEREIGN DELUXE

Attractive and economically-priced curved eaves conservatories with unusually low ridge height to suit practically all situations. Both models have sturdy aluminium framework in a choice of brown or white maintenance-free finishes and the door position can be at either end of the building. Toughened safety glass is used throughout except for the curved eaves (which are in stay-clear acrylic) – and roof and gable ventilation are standard features. These conservatories are available in depths of 6ft or 8ft and in lengths of 8ft, 10ft or 12ft. Any of these lengths can also be increased in multiples of 6ft by using extension modules. The main difference between the two models is that the Sovereign has spring glazing clips, whereas the Sovereign Deluxe uses continuous plastic glazing strips for enhanced appearance. Also, both depths of the Sovereign have a single sliding door, whereas the 8ft deep Sovereign Deluxe has a double sliding door.

THE BACO NEW LEISURE ROOM

An economically-priced aluminium conservatory with variable ridge height, making it ideal for homes with low eaves or partly tiled walls which restrict the height available. This building – introduced for the 1988 season – is an improved and restyled version of the original Leisure Room, which it supersedes. Finished in a choice of maintenance-free white or brown, the New Leisure Room has top hung windows and residential-style single or double doors (sealed all round) which can be fitted in a variety of positions. Glazing is in full length toughened glass panels for maximum safety. The New Leisure Room is available in depths of 6ft 4in or 8ft 5in and in lengths of 8ft 4in or 10ft 4in.

THE HALLS GARDEN LOUNGE

This is an economically-priced aluminium building with hinged double doors – lockable from inside or out – in the front wall. It is available in a choice of white or brown maintenance-free finishes and in three length options (9ft 10in, 12ft 4in or 14ft 9in) – all in a single depth of 7ft 7in. Standard features include louvred ventilators fitted in each gable, plus concealed rainwater guttering. For maximum safety, full-length toughened glass is used throughout and is secured onto weatherproof uPVC cushion seals by attractive continuous beading.

THE BANBURY SUNBURY

The Sunbury has long been a favourite and, despite its economical price, it is constructed in pre-treated prime Western red cedar, which is inherently rot resistant. The lower walls are in immensely strong pressed concrete in a choice of four attractive exterior finishes and are lined internally. Windows and doors are fitted with toughened glass for extra safety and the roof is either tough uPVC sheeting or – new for 1988 – twin skin polycarbonate. Four top-hung windows are included as standard and the door can be positioned at either end of the conservatory. The Sunbury is available in seven lengths up to 17ft 6in and in a single depth of 6ft.

THE EDEN TROPIQUE

This robust and distinctively-styled aluminium conservatory features attractive curved eaves and has double sliding patio doors (with high security lock) in the front wall. It is available in a choice of white or brown maintenance-free finishes. Standard features include ridge ventilation and, for maximum safety, full length toughened glazing panels are used throughout. If required, a single residential door can be incorporated in one or both ends. The Tropique is available in depths of 8ft 2in or 10ft 2in and in six lengths from 10ft 4in to 20ft 5in.

THE EDEN ELAN

The Elan is an established favourite featuring glass-to-ground styling, sharply curved solid eaves and neat, uncluttered design. As with all conservatories available from Banbury, safety glazing is used throughout. The maintenance-free aluminium alloy frame is finished in a choice of brown or white and a residential side door – lockable from inside and out – is included in the standard specification. Depths of 8ft 3in and 10ft 3in are available, and six lengths to 20ft 7in.

THE EDEN CAMARGUE

The Camargue's distinctive, uncluttered good looks have made it one of Britain's best selling conservatories. Available in a choice of white or brown finishes, its robust aluminium framework is maintenance-free and there is an easy-glide sliding patio door (with security locking) in the front wall. In addition, the building can be supplied with a high quality hinged residential door in one end if required. The glazing is glass-to-ground style and is in toughened glass for maximum safety. A new feature for 1988 is that the glass has been made more difficult to remove by intruders. The Camargue is available in depths of 8ft 3in or 10ft 3in and in five lengths from 10ft 6in to 18ft 7in.

THE EDEN MISTRAL

Modern, uncluttered styling and a low ridge that is especially suitable for fitting onto bungalows – these are the hallmarks of the Mistral Conservatory. Combining style with security, it has easy-glide sliding patio doors with high security locking and attractively-styled handles. The robust aluminium framework can be in white or brown maintenance-free finish and a high performance casement window is included at each end of the building. A hinged residential door, opening outwards, is also available on either side if required. As on all conservatories available from Banbury, the Mistral is safety glazed throughout. Models are available in depths of 8ft 7in or 10ft 6in, and six lengths from 10ft 6in to 20ft 5in.

THE HALLS LASER

Incorporating all the time-honoured traditions of a true conservatory, the Laser is another model new to the Banbury range. Its immensely strong box section aluminium frame is available in a choice of white or brown maintenance-free finishes. Double sliding doors are provided in the front wall and the Laser can also have a single sliding door in one or both ends if required. As with all conservatories available from Banbury, toughened glass is a standard feature. Laser models are available in a single depth of 7ft 5in and in lengths of 10ft, 12ft 6in or 14ft 11in. In addition, length extensions are available in multiples of 4ft 10in.

THE BANBURY TRADITIONAL

The Traditional has been one of Banbury's most popular conservatories for a long time. Its strong and durable concrete walls (in a choice of attractive finishes) support a main frame in rot-inhibiting red cedar which blends with any garden setting. Features include a twin skin safety roof, internal lining, skirting boards, security ventilation, guttering and adjustable door restraints. Originally available in depths of 7ft 9in and 9ft 4in, with seven lengths up to 24ft 5in, the range has recently been extended by the addition of a 6ft depth available in the same length options.

THE ROOM 2000 GALAXIE

The Galaxie is one of the newest additions to the Banbury range and is one of the most versatile conservatories on the market. It can be single glazed or sealed unit double glazed and in the latter case is economical to heat for use as a fully habitable home extension. In all cases toughened safety glass is used. The heavy gauge maintenance-free aluminium framework can be in white, brown, mushroom or cream, or any two-tone combination of these colours. The Galaxie has a hinged residential-style door in the end of your choice and a top-hung casement window in the other end. Optional extras include sliding patio doors in the front wall, acrylic roof vents which can be fitted between any or all of the glazing bars, and control gear which gives fingertip adjustment to the roof vents. Standard Galaxie models are available in depths of 8ft, 10ft, 12ft and 14ft, and in six lengths from 10ft 9in to 21ft. Alternatively, 'tailor-made' options are available in the exact size and layout required.

THE BACO SUMMER ROOM

The Summer Room features four attractive 'Bell-shaped' styles including elegant 'Victorian' models. With options including single or double safety glazing, Summer Room models are in high-grade aluminium enhanced by an exterior cladding of white uPVC. This is attractive, maintenance-free and super-insulating, so heat loss – and therefore condensation – is substantially reduced. Special attention has also been paid to ventilation, with an easily operated ventilated cowl – built into the roof apex – for use with or instead of door and window ventilation. Other features include concealed rainwater disposal and an absolutely smooth interior and exterior finish without screws, buts or bolts being visible. All Summer Room models are available in a choice of sizes.

THE EDEN CORNICHE

The Corniche – a recent addition to the Banbury range – is a luxury conservatory of extreme versatility. For a start it is available in both standard height or 'bungalow height' versions. It has sealed unit double glazed walls, a triple skin polycarbonate roof and thermally broken aluminium framework – making it economical to heat for fully habitable use. Then there's versatility of layout. Front walls with a choice of double sliding patio or double leaf residential doors; and ends that can be fitted with residential doors, casement windows, or just left plain. Naturally, all doors and opening windows have thermal barrier frames and the doors are fitted with multi-point locks as standard. As you'd expect, the Corniche's gleaming white finish is maintenance-free and the sealed glazing units are in toughened glass held in place with high security glazing beads. Corniche models are available in depths of 8ft 6in or 11ft 3in, and in five lengths from 10ft 6in to 20ft 9in. They can also be supplied as two sided buildings for corner fitting.

THE ROOM 2000 GEMINI

Another recent addition to Banbury's range is the Gemini – a luxurious conservatory available in a wide choice of standard options or 'tailor-made' in the exact size and layout of your choice. Even standard Gemini models are outstandingly versatile, with options including a shallow roof pitch version for building onto bungalows; four widths from 8ft to 14ft; six lengths from 10ft to 20ft; sliding patio doors in the front; ends that can include sliding patio doors, residential doors or top hung windows; and clear or bronze tinted roof. All Gemini models are sealed unit double glazed and have thermal barrier aluminium framework, making them economical to heat for fully habitable use all year round. Standard colour options are white, brown, mushroom or cream and a vast range of other colours are available to special order. Naturally, the framework is maintenance-free.

Corniche

THE BANBURY VICTORIANA

The Victoriana is a 'Bell' style conservatory in Western Red Cedar – a timber renowned for its inherent resistance to rot. It is available either single glazed or, to make it economical to heat for fully habitable year-round use, it can be sealed unit double glazed. Either way, toughened safety glass is used throughout and there's a choice of six attractive window styles, all available in full height versions with relief carved lower panels, or without the lower panels for building onto a brick or stone dwarf wall. Double doors with solid brass fittings are a standard feature and can be fitted in virtually any position. The Victoriana has a minimum of two opening roof vents and all models have hinged and fixed side windows alternating along the building's length. Dentil moulding and ridge cresting are also available. The Victoriana is 12ft 1in wide and there are seven depth options from 8ft 8in to 23ft 1in.

THE HALLMARK SENATOR

Another recent Banbury addition is the Senator – a high quality timber conservatory which can be tailored to meet individual customer needs and an almost limitless range of applications. Available in Mahogany hardwood or vacuum-treated softwood, it can be single glazed, or sealed unit double glazed for full use all year round. It can be 'glass to ground' style or have moulded timber lower panels; and the twin skin safety roof can be clear or bronze tinted. Quite apart from 'tailor-made' options, the Senator's modular design enables a very wide range of sizes to be produced from standard components. It also allows a single or double sliding door (depending on conservatory size) to be fitted in the front wall and/or a single sliding door to be fitted in either or both ends. Ventilation is provided by highly efficient controllable concealed ventilators at eaves level. The Senator is available in three depths of 6ft 6in, 7ft 11in, or 9ft 7in and, depending on depth, in nine lengths from 6ft 10in to 32ft 0in.

THE HALLMARK CONSORT

The Consort – also recently added to Banbury's range – is similar to the Senator (see previous page) except that it has a shallower roof pitch, giving a ridge height of only 7ft 6in for building onto bungalows and houses where there is a height restriction. Instead of vents built into the eaves as on the Senator, the Consort's ventilation is provided by one or more side opening windows fitted with high quality security handles and friction stays. Additionally, there is the option of arch-topped windows instead of rectangular ones to further enhance the appearance. The roof on the Consort is twin-skin clear polycarbonate and a suspended translucent sun ceiling is fitted to diffuse strong summer sunlight. In all other respects the Consort is identical to the Senator and all the same options apply.

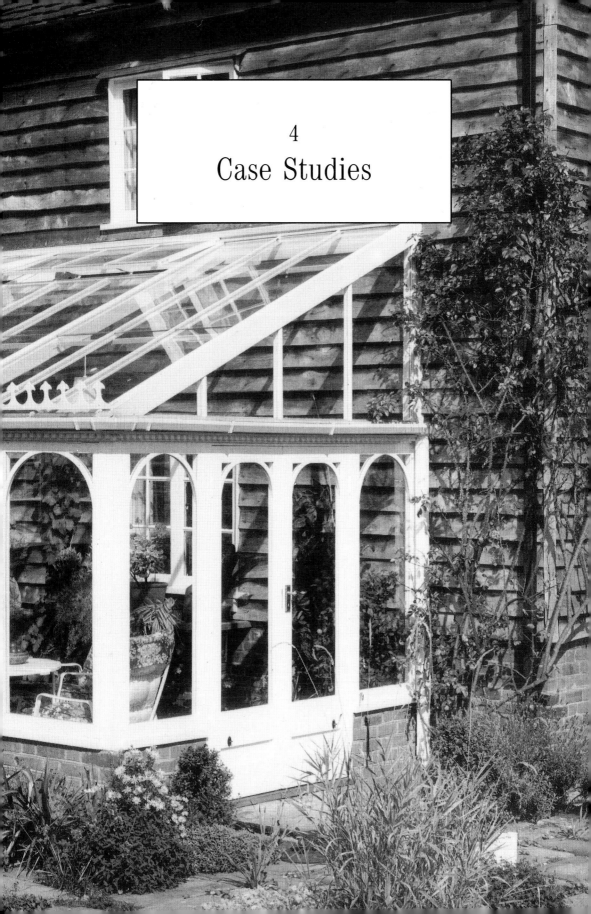

4
Case Studies

Fig 34 Amdega's octagonal conservatory

PREVIOUS PAGE:

Close-up of lean-to conservatory on page 45, complete with MSH/MSR sashes, and eaves cresting.

Picture an apricot sun climbing out of the North Sea aiming shafts of watery summer sunlight along the Tyne Valley and speeding with them the promise of a gloriously warm day for those fortunate enough to be living in the magnificent area around Corbridge in Northumbria. What better way to greet such an exhilarating morning than over breakfast in your own conservatory?

One particularly delightful home near Corbridge – perhaps some dozen miles from Newcastle – provides the Victorian interpretation of an earlier vernacular style. This is a substantial, stone-built farmhouse. Domestic architecture used designs which provided comfortable family accommodation while resisting the bleakest weather conditions this area can conjure up during its winters. This farmhouse is sited 400 to 500ft (122 to 152m) above sea level on the northern slope of the valley carved out by the Tyne between the foothills of the north Pennines and south Cheviots, and is therefore at latitudes which place it almost within javelin throwing distance of Hadrian's Wall. And having witnessed the area in virtually all its seasons, it is easy to sympathise with the attitude of the 'wall soldier' who during the Roman occupation of the region bemoaned his lot in that well known poem by E. E. Cummings. Given this meteorological and topographical scenario, the decision to build a conservatory in such a location might at first appear absurd. But then again, there are plenty more conservatories at more northerly latitudes than this. What is remarkable is that compared to the 13in (33cm) thick stone walls of the house, the relative lightness of this double-glazed structure in fact renders it no more vulnerable to rough weather than is the house itself.

This particular house stands then on an elevated site enjoying unrivalled views of the local countryside, and is set in its own grounds. The mature garden is carefully terraced and includes areas set to lawn, all screened from the kitchen garden by a majestic beech hedge. Below this upper level is a tennis court and landscaped garden separated only by a drystone wall from the paddock beyond, this in its turn sweeps gently down to the edge of an ornamental lake frequented by wild deer and water birds. This is a delightful micro-landscape and the conservatory optimises the enjoyment of it by offering something like a 270° panoramic vistadome to watch it from as it goes through its myriad transitions of mood. The conservatory is an agreeable way of extending your home out into your garden, but in this Corbridge example it allows the occupants to enjoy a much closer relationship with their natural environment as well.

Romantic? Whimsical? The image possibly is.

The creative solution – an architect designed conservatory constructed between stable block and house.

CASE STUDY 1

Who would ever have suspected that within a few hundred yards of a bustling market centre, an all but overgrown lane concealed the entrance to a charming country home? Yet that is precisely the situation to be found on the Cambridge road leading eastwards out of St Neots. What is now an island of tranquillity set within this busy urban envelope may once have been a seventeenth-century farmstead. The history of the building merits several paragraphs of consideration in a publication entitled *St. Neots. History of a Huntingdonshire Town* by C. F. Tebbutt. Despite the uncertainty of its origins, however, this delightful old redbrick house, known locally as Goodlands, now sits at the centre of almost two acres of lawned gardens and mature trees, among which a few rows of grape vines may be glimpsed.

At the beginning of the eighteenth century, the house was separated from a small stable block by a courtyard. About four years ago the present owners implemented a scheme to integrate the house with the stable block and enclose the courtyard at the same time. The creative solution to this particular structural problem was an architect-designed conservatory which could form two sides of a linking building and could also tie into a tiled roof section – intended to match the existing roofs – that would be constructed between stable block and house. The main elevation of the proposed conservatory would contain a significant amount of single glazing set at a remarkably steep angle of pitch. Asked to consider this architectural problem at least one major manufacturer of conservatories was unable to meet these somewhat testing specifications, but Amdega rose to the challenge and provided a rather special conservatory that now forms a light and spacious living area harmonising beautifully with the rest of this Grade Two listed building. Working in close liaison with the architect for the project, Amdega was able to supply this conservatory which had been in place almost two years when the accompanying photographs were taken. The conservatory was transported from the Darlington factory to the site ready for the building firm contracted by the owners to erect. A concrete base had already been laid, and once the entire building incorporating the conservatory had been completed its concrete floor was covered with hard-wearing, industrial rubber tiles. With three children in the family, this newly created room was intended for use as an additional living room. Although it has not quite achieved this purpose, this very delightful conservatory room – flanked on both sides by prolific lawns and flower beds – is in daily use as a family dining area.

CASE STUDY 2

The Chiltern hills are a delightful area in which to live, boasting a rich variety of domestic architecture. Alison and Norman Sharp have an attractive home – one of two semi-detached properties completed by a local builder sometime in the 1930s as gardeners' cottages, but much extended since. After fourteen years the Sharps began to feel the need for additional living space, but did not want to move to a larger house. As with so many other purchasers of conservatories, progressively escalating property prices was one of the main factors taken into consideration in making a decision to add a conservatory to provide that extra space. There were at least two other considerations of equal, if not greater importance. With a property of this character on an elevated site, the Sharps enjoy superb views with a vista of some fifteen to twenty miles rolling towards Oxford. It is even possible to make out the buildings of Lady Spencer Churchill College on a reasonably clear day. Also their house is extremely convenient for Norman Sharp's place of work, which is just a few minutes away.

Having made the decision to add a conservatory to their home rather than move to a larger property, Alison and Norman spent some time considering costs, visual appearance and materials. They finally decided to buy an Amdega model because they felt that this particular style, in wood rather than aluminium, was the most sympathetic to the vernacular character of their house. Their particular conservatory is an Amdega special. It is double glazed and centrally heated for two main reasons – the structure is sited on the north side of the house, which itself is in an elevated position, so the conservatory is inevitably quite cold because it is comparatively exposed. In this area of Buckinghamshire there is invariably snow in the winter months, and temperatures are consistently a few degrees lower than those experienced in the towns and villages on the plain below. There is also a significant wind chill factor that cannot be overlooked.

While the Sharps engaged a local builder to put in the base and the walls, Norman himself undertook to erect the conservatory. Probably few people would want to take on such a challenge, but Norman found that the plans and instructions supplied by Amdega were not at all difficult to follow. Erecting the timber framework took only a week

OPPOSITE

A spacious interior is created by Amdega for a house in Weybridge, Surrey. This conservatory combines special and modular sections and is double glazed and comprises two octagonals of the same size on either side of a lean-to.

This particular style, realised in wood rather than aluminium, was the most sympathetic to the vernacular character of the house.

to complete, followed by the glazing which took rather longer. After a couple of years the conservatory has come to serve several different purposes. Alison Sharp uses it as a sewing room because the quality of the light is so good. It forms part of a complex including a patio area and a barbecue pit, so that when the Sharp family decides to cook and eat alfresco, it can act as a useful shelter should the weather be less than perfect. The quarry-tiled floor is therefore particularly appropriate, being hard wearing and easily cleaned, which is just as well since the Sharps are both keen gardeners, too. Alison has an eyecatching variety of plants in hanging baskets as well as in pots on the floor and window-sill staging. Worthy of particular mention is the Hoya vine whose flowers literally drip nectar that in its native habitat would be the target for humming birds, and there are planters containing orchids in abundance. The juxtaposition of these plants with simple cane furniture is one that seems to work particularly well. Most of all, however, this extra living room has become a kind of parents' refuge – especially on Sundays when Norman and Alison retreat into their conservatory with a glass of wine and their Sunday newspapers to enjoy a quiet read, and of course those wonderful views across the countryside below towards Oxford.

OPPOSITE

A professionally arranged bench display in the Stewart Park conservatory, Middlesbrough, Cleveland, featuring an air layered ficus in the background with irisine, browalia, primula, chlorophytum, hedera helix and small begonia.

The setting for this conservatory is sublime with a croquet lawn and formal garden patrolled by a peacock and his mate.

CASE STUDY 3

Not only do the Chilterns feature some superb houses, there is also a wealth of fascinating village names such as Bledlow Ridge, Lacey Green, Parslows Hillock and Loosley Row – and this is the country-side of the remarkable Ridgeway footpath. These rural parishes harbour their fair share of conservatories, and there is one in par-ticular attached to a charming Victorian cottage close to a public house going by the unusual name of The Pink and Lily. Here again the distinctively Victorian appearance of an Amdega conservatory blends particularly well with the original architectural style of the cottage. And with four other similar conservatories by the same manufacturer owned by other members of the family the choice was almost inevitable. The setting for this conservatory is sublime with a view across perhaps an acre of formal garden with a croquet lawn towards a further acre of woodland. Several species of birds roam the grounds including a very splendid peacock and his mate.

This single-glazed model – erected by a local builder – had been in situ almost two years when it was visited by the author. With central heating (extended to it from the domestic system) and a floor of hexagonal quarry tiles imported from Wales and covered with rush matting squares, this garden room is uniquely furnished with cane chairs made by those disciples of meditation at nearby Mentmore Towers. The owners of this conservatory, William and Jane, say they almost live in it for eight to nine months of the year. Being quite high up in the Chilterns there are not very many days when it is warm enough to sit out in the garden. Inside the conservatory with its south-east facing aspect it is quite another story – the owners have all their meals there and continue to take Saturday and Sunday lunches in it right through into November. They have deliberately not installed any electric lighting, preferring to use just candles which creates a more subtle, sotto voce quality of light that somehow complements the evening outside.

It needs very little sunlight to raise the temperature within this conservatory quite dramatically. Consequently the attachment of self-opening devices to the roof lights was a very prudent addition. One omission, though, was the lack of blinds that would have helped diffuse some of the glare of direct sunlight. Being very enthusiastic gardeners, Jane and husband William have seized the opportunity to furnish their conservatory with numerous plants – abutilon, morning glory, tradescantia and chlorophytum along with geraniums thrive particularly well and these all contribute to a most inviting recreational space enclosed by glass.

CASE STUDY 4

Across the vale from the Chiltern hills the city of Oxford contains numerous substantial town houses. One property, in a row of half pebble-dashed semi-detached Edwardian villas, has a rare example of a detached conservatory within its walled and secluded garden at the back. Sited approximately west to east this conservatory has its main elevation facing south thereby taking maximum advantage of whatever sunshine may be available. The choice of a conservatory – distinctively an Amdega model – represented an elegant solution to the need for a plant house without having to resort to the more utilitarian design typical of a greenhouse. Amdega design was preferred because it allowed the flexibility of form needed to fit into the space available without incurring a level of cost that would have proved prohibitive. The distance from the house to the conservatory meant that extending the domestic central heating system was really not a viable proposition. But since it was primarily intended as a controllable environment for raising plants there was a need for some kind of heating. Electricity has been laid on, for lighting and to power a thermostatically-controlled fan-blown heating unit, and there are additional power points. One omission initially was the decision not to include blinds, but this has since been rectified.

Although detached, this conservatory is a little unusual in that it has two brick walls on its north and east elevations rising to the height of its eaves. What in consequence it may lose in light penetration is, however, more than compensated for by having a roof with a central ridge with glass pitches on either side. The conservatory is set in a sunken patio area paved in weathered red brick arranged in a very attractive herring-bone pattern and surrounded by a low retaining wall. This glazed pavilion serves a twofold function. It is decidedly traditional in its use as a protective environment for overwintering precious plants that are returned to the garden outdoors in the summer season. A jasmine vine dominates the north wall and alongside it a lobster claw – *clianthus punicens* – provides an abundance of red flowers. Abutilon, fuchsias, geraniums and morning glory are all well in evidence in their season, occupying considerable floor space in a variety of earthenware tubs and pots, and this is a favourite place for raising tomatoes. The structure is also ideal for sitting in at leisure and for taking meals, and for this reason instead of loading the window-sill staging with plants, here it has been converted to use as window seating instead. The owners particularly enjoy taking morning coffee or afternoon tea in their conservatory, and have equipped themselves with a remote telephone so that there is no need to rush back to the house to answer incoming calls.

Considering its main use as a plant-raising environment, a floor laid with quarry tiles recommends itself as a very serviceable solution. Again, considering the detached position of the conservatory, the use of self-opening devices on all the roof lights reduces the necessity for frequent visits to open or close casements so as to regulate temperatures and air circulation.

A rather superior greenhouse . . .

CASE STUDY 5

On the edge of a small village on the outskirts of the university city of Cambridge, within a few miles of Impington Village College designed by German Bauhaus architect Walther Gropius, is a mid-1930s bungalow that has undergone a programme of rejuvenation. This bungalow has been in the same family for two generations – it belonged to the father of the present head of household – which accounts for the depth of care and concern that went into its revitalisation. The main priority was to retain as much of the original character of the building as possible, yet upgrade the house to domestic standards appropriate to the late 1980s. It was, for example, necessary to renew all the roof timbers. This project was accomplished by the careful removal of the original roof tiles. The timbers beneath were replaced, and the tiles were then refitted exactly as they had been first fixed more than half a century before.

Keeping to their original intention of refurbishing this property without overtly modernising it, when the owners decided to add extra living space to their home they rejected the idea of a conventional brick-built extension with a flat roof. This they felt would detract from the character of their bungalow and would add no value to it either. They soon decided that a conservatory would provide the solution to their requirement for additional space. They already had one of sorts, built soon after the 1939/45 war, but it was in very poor condition and unsuitably sited to enclose the back door. They initially drew up their own plans for a conservatory, and submitted a plan for approval, only to discover later in a country interest magazine a design remarkably similar to the one they had already visualised themselves. It was an Amdega product.

Planning permission had been applied for and granted some three years before their discovery of this Amdega design. By 1982 alterations to the original plan had been agreed by the local authority and the conservatory project was ready to proceed. It was, however, almost a further year before the owner was able to finish digging the footings himself. A builder was then contracted and the conservatory from Amdega was erected by October 1985. It is part of a comprehensive plan that also includes refurbishment of kitchen, garage and utility room areas, and has itself several unusual features. In order to preserve the integrity of the original architecture, especially its symmetry, the conservatory has been erected precisely on the central axis of the bungalow at the rear, and has been integrated into the existing roof structure by means of a hip, which confers a pleasing roofline to the whole shape of the building. Unlike most other domestic conservatories, the floor is timber which not only matches the timber floor of the bungalow itself, but also facilitates the airflow beneath the floor joists of the entire building.

As this conservatory is intended to function primarily as a year-round living space it is double glazed, which in turn helps improve the insulation qualities of the bungalow's rear elevation which faces due east. Central heating has not been extended from the bungalow; the conservatory has its own storage heater for use over the winter period. Maintaining adequate temperatures throughout the year is important for the vine that is being trained to grow up one corner. This vine is actually planted in a brick-lined bed outside the conservatory, and enters the conservatory through a purpose-built duct in the dwarf wall; the wall is lined with glass-fibre wool to discourage rodent penetration to the interior and subsequently to the bungalow itself. According to the owners, the reason for planting the vine outside is that these plants are greedy feeders and are much easier to manage successfully if rooted in an outdoor bed.

The vine has been introduced into the conservatory through a purpose designed duct in the dwarf wall.

In recent years conservatories have come to be regarded as fashionable additions to a home. This is a modular special conservatory, comprising of two modular lean-tos back to back with special octagonal front section.

CASE STUDY 6

Not far from the East Anglian town of Wisbech is a standard Amdega conservatory that had already been in use for a couple of years when it was visited by the author. In contrast to the more practical reasons underlying most decisions to purchase a conservatory, for Malcolm and Susan they were essentially aesthetic. It is undeniably the case that in recent years conservatories have come to be regarded as fashionable additions to homes, a view which complements the earlier and more utilitarian consideration inherited from the late 1960s, when they were seen primarily as inexpensive additional rooms. The conservatory described here has been added to an already spacious house with the express intention of making the rear elevation of the property more pleasing to the eye. It is intended mainly for seasonal use – for relaxing in and entertaining, like a gazebo or summer house – and is consequently only single glazed, unheated and without sun screening.

Malcolm engaged his own builder to put up the dwarf walls and erect the conservatory. One particularly interesting feature is evident in the brickwork – handmade 'Tudor' bricks – and is related to the hexagonal form of the structure: vertical joints in the brickwork where the wall sections intersect have been carefully avoided by the clever use of pre-formed angled bricks. These squint bricks confer two distinct advantages: they provide the dwarf walls with more strength, and obviate any tendency to produce unsightly joints.

ILLUSTRATED ON PP 144–5

CASE STUDY 7

They had had one before, a conservatory that is. All the houses in the surrounding nineteenth-century terraces had had small conservatories as an integral part of their original design. Today, the fabric of the majority of these structures has deteriorated to such an extent they have become susceptible to the elements, are no longer weatherproof and are often in so poor a state of repair they are beyond revitalisation. Having been in their present home some seven years, the owners of this delightful, late Victorian terraced property in London's Chiswick area decided they enjoyed their dilapidated conservatory so much that it should be replaced by a new one, and preferably a conservatory that would blend with the character of their home. Thoughts turned first to an individual design. An architect was duly commissioned and although the ensuing blueprints were exquisite in detail, some of the intricate joinery would have been difficult to realise and the structure's estimated cost proved to be prohibitive. Consequently the plans never got off the drawing board and the project was abandoned.

A search then began to find a conservatory manufacturer not only capable of providing a design sympathetic to the architectural style, but also able to erect the conservatory as well. The project was started in late May, a local builder contracted to put in the base and by mid-August the conservatory was in place and completed at a cost of approximately £100 per sq ft (.09sq m) (1986). Anyone who supports the philosophy asserting 'small is beautiful' cannot fail to be charmed by this Bartholomew conservatory. Occupying slightly more than 62sq ft (5.58sq m) in area it is the smallest conservatory visited by the author in the course of researching this book, yet its form satisfies its function more perfectly than many of its grander counterparts. The house to which it is attached dates from 1892, so its architecture is complemented by the Bartholomew design, which itself is inspired by late Victorian and Edwardian style. As much pleasure can be derived from the aesthetic appeal of the structure as from the quality of materials and craftsmanship. One of the advantages of this particular design is that it does not require dwarf walls, so the amount of pre-requisite building work is limited to just a base. The rest of the construction is dry – an important consideration when all building materials must be brought in through the house because there is no access from the rear.

This conservatory meets several needs. Primarily it functions as an extra room on the back of the house where it provides a new aspect opening onto the delightful walled garden. Facing due south the conservatory enjoys the seasonal benefit of sun throughout the day, and is consequently well lit – a matter that really calls for some sort of

*A*nyone who supports the philosophy asserting 'small is beautiful' cannot fail to be charmed by this Bartholomew conservatory.

screening which the structure initially lacked. Although it is not centrally heated, the conservatory is double glazed making it a cosy and comfortable space in which to work – Alison is a writer and works from home – as well as a place to entertain and relax. Moreover, being double glazed the conservatory affords a degree of protection to the rear of this property and raises the level of security. Even in winter it requires only minimal heat which is provided by a small oil-filled electric radiator. At least one of the owners is an exceptionally keen gardener. But because there is relatively little space available at floor level, there is really nowhere to stand plants, and window staging could only be erected at the expense of sitting room. The problem of how to include plants like a grape vine, hibiscus, fuchsias, jasmine and geraniums has been ingeniously resolved by having picture-rail shelving for potted plants, and suspending additional plants in hanging baskets. The variety blends most effectively to provide an attractive display and helps create a most inviting environment.

CASE STUDY 8

Judging purely by external appearances David's Bartholomew conservatory had been added to a very pleasing example of vernacular architecture dating back who could guess how many years? All of which goes to show how deceptive appearances can be as regards domestic architecture because this particular cottage had been built not long after World War I, by a local builder it is true – hence the vernacular touch perhaps – and was consequently barely of pensionable age. It is no less delightful for all this, set in its own mature gardens on the fringe of a Berkshire village bordering the Thames not far from Maidenhead. In its sixty or so years the cottage has been extended twice. On both occasions the work has been carried through in such a way as to remain truthful to the original architecture. In their turn David and his wife, the present owners, wished to add more space. But right from the start, their first concern was that whatever form of extension might ultimately be commissioned it had to be most carefully considered so that it would not conflict with the prevailing style of the building. First thoughts had been to move to a larger house; second thoughts favoured the idea of adding a conservatory to their present home that would confer not merely additional space, but light and air as well.

An architect was engaged for the project and it was decided that the shape of the existing patio at the rear of the cottage, with its south-facing aspect, should determine the floor plan of the structure.

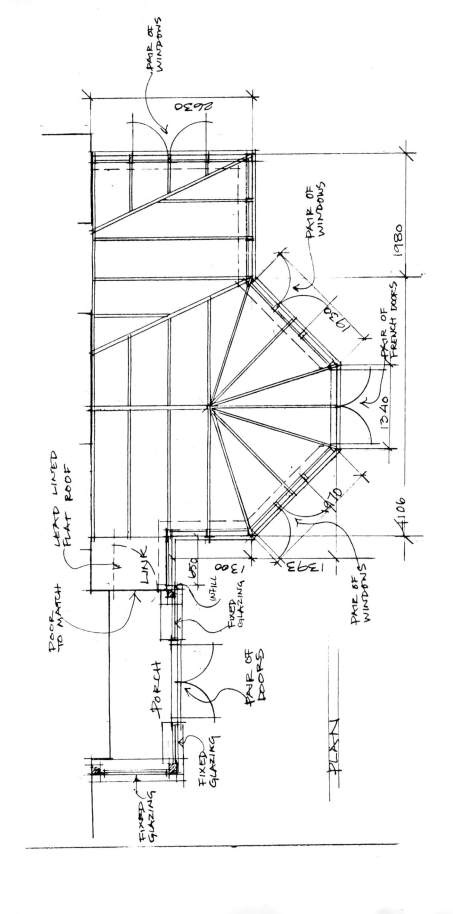

PAIR OF WINDOWS

2630

PAIR OF WINDOWS

1980

PAIR OF FRENCH DOORS

1030

1340

4106

470

1393

1300

650 (INFILL)

FIXED GLAZING

PAIR OF WINDOWS

LEAD LINED FLAT ROOF

DOOR TO MATCH

LINK

PORCH

PAIR OF DOORS

FIXED GLAZING

FIXED GLAZING

PLAN

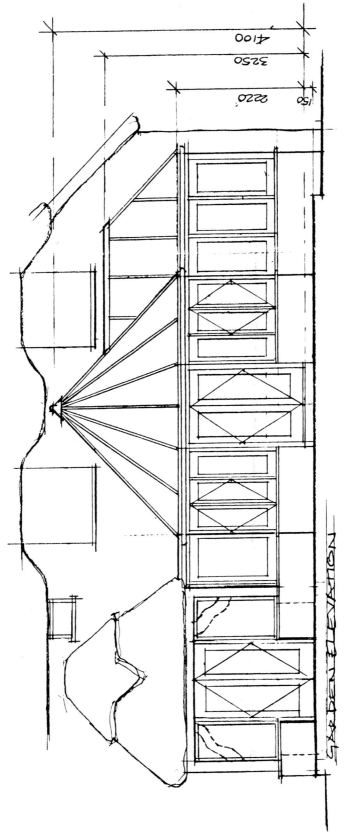

4100
3250
2220'
150

GARDEN ELEVATION

Figs 35 & 36 Bartholomew plan and garden elevation for the conservatory at Cookham Thatch

This Bartholomew conservatory, patio and mature garden combine to constitute an organic design concept (see interior on following pages).

Basically the patio has been enclosed within a glass envelope. But it was also felt that a conservatory can be incongruous if erected and left to stand in isolation. They really do beg to be 'landscaped' into their surroundings; to be linked to a garden by means of a patio, so for David's conservatory this required the construction of a new patio.

At its highest point the structure reaches all of 12ft (3.6m) up to the eaves of the cottage roof. In their concern to ensure the conservatory did not in any way detract visually from their property, the same angle of pitch as the cottage roof has been maintained. Additionally, the cottage features some dark timber work – decorative rather than structural – so the owners were at pains to match the woodwork of the new conservatory in hue and tone to the muted original as nearly as possible so that the new structure did not jar the eye. The external walls of the cottage were rendered at this time to help sustain the rural character of the entire cottage/conservatory structure.

This conservatory is double glazed, with side-hinged casements but no roof vents. Nor does it have any form of sunlight screening, something the owners have come to recognise as an oversight. Roof vents and screens are both items commonly overlooked by many at the time of ordering. With a comparatively large roof section, the conservatory tends to trap a considerable amount of heat on sunny days which cannot be vented easily to the outside. A large fan suspended from the roof timbers certainly helps stir the air within into some measure of movement. Even so it seemed quite possible that it could easily become too warm for comfort. But David defends this by asking who would want to remain indoors under glass on a warm, sunny day in summer anyway? Surprisingly perhaps, although the structure boasts three radiators fed from the domestic central heating system the owners felt it still needed additional heating from a portable source in the winter months. Declaring no special purpose for their conservatory, David and his wife have nonetheless furnished it quite fully with matching table, chairs and suite, designating it as the best place for casual lunches at weekends, or for sitting out in the evenings to enjoy coffee and conversation with friends. As well as its furnishings this conservatory features a particularly attractive floor of polished marble aggregate tiles laid on a diagonal to the lines of the structure itself in order to counter any tendency to over-emphasise intersecting right angles, which would make for geometrical harshness. Ultimately the entire project, conservatory and patio together with the mature garden, expresses precisely what the owners intended, and is a nice example of an overall design that constitutes an organic concept.

CASE STUDY 9

When the owners of a pre-war (1937) house in Bushey Heath, Hertfordshire, decided to invest in a conservatory, they bought with it a major headache because local authority planners insisted on exceptionally deep foundations. There was an inherent difficulty to be overcome anyway, involving the significant difference in level between the ground floor of the house and the garden below because of the property's elevated site. This necessitated a considerable amount of building up from the garden level several feet below to construct a patio. But planning permission plumbed new depths. It was granted on condition the foundations for the conservatory were dug to more than 10ft (3m) below the planned floor level of the conservatory itself. Having weathered this initial problem, the entire family is delighted with the resulting structure, a Bartholomew design which is used principally for growing and conserving plants which surround a central area designated for sitting and relaxing. Plants favoured by Carol include jasmine, plumbago, oleander, citrus, ficus and fuchsias. Also successfully tried have been tomatoes, green peppers and cucumbers. But although these fruits and vegetables thrived it was found they tended to attract insects such as whitefly and greenfly into the conservatory that became something of a nuisance. It is also Carol's experience that the environment is not particularly forgiving where ferns are concerned. They tend not to fare too well and are susceptible to sun-scorching on leaves. Again perhaps, this argues strongly for the inclusion of some form of sun-screening. Although double glazed, this conservatory is not centrally heated and winter temperatures as low as 40°F (4°C) have been recorded, causing cold damage to plants placed too close to the glazing – particularly citrus varieties. This is a kind of irony, bearing in mind that the forerunner of today's modern conservatory – the Orangery – was devised as the solution to overwintering fashionable orange and lemon bushes.

That a conservatory is considered fashionable, and as adding value to a property are two additional reasons advanced by Ronnie and Carol for making their purchase. An exceptionally pleasing suspended wooden floor stamps a distinctly domestic personality on this particular conservatory, which is tightly integrated into the house itself, cradled between kitchen and lounge with doors opening from the conservatory into both of these areas. Much debate ranges around what may constitute the perfect floor surface for a conservatory, and while a sealed, polished wooden floor may not be quite as practical as, say, quarry tiles, it is somehow softer, warmer and more cosy. That said, it does require additional attention because it is prone to water damage. Great care is taken when watering the profusion of plants ranged around the edges of this garden room.

Carol and Ronnie are unusual in that they devote their conservatory much more to plants than many other owners. This is chiefly because they and their children delight in sitting amongst their plants, sometimes listening to music, and find it really helps them relax. Cane furniture – chairs, table, settee and stools upholstered in green velvet – is in perfect harmony with the wealth of plants that serve to orchestrate the space. The entire family enjoys the conservatory and all confess themselves pleased with this addition to their home. In constant use from May to October, evenings will often find Carol and Ronnie in their conservatory playing bridge with friends. But on those all too rare sunny days this is definitely no summer house to sit in, and was never intended as such. However in winter with a covering of snow the conservatory beckons as an agreeable environment and may then be considered more of a winter house than a summer one.

From the point of view of maintenance no problems have been experienced since the structure was erected. This includes such mundane matters as window cleaning – even keeping the roof panels free of any rain-staining. The structure has proved solid enough for the local window cleaner to work his way across the roof with chamois leather by making use of the timbers.

The entire family is delighted with this Bartholomew design for this family home in Bushey Heath.

Conservatories often provide interesting examples of flexibility in design.

CASE STUDY 10

When they moved from their Georgian house in Cambridgeshire to a spacious bungalow set in its own mature and carefully planned gardens just outside Harpenden, Lawrence and Robin knew their living room led into a sun lounge of sorts. Although the previous owners of the bungalow had been very keen gardeners and had filled this so-called sun lounge with plants, both Robin and her husband also knew that this rather jaded timber structure would have to be replaced – and fairly quickly. They decided to replace the sun lounge extension with a conservatory, and having looked at several manufacturers each offering a variety of alternatives the couple decided a design by Amdega would be best suited to their particular property. Drawing on a lifetime of experience as a planning officer with local authorities, Lawrence concluded that a standard Amdega design enclosing approximately 625sq ft (56.25sq m) of floor area would meet their needs. He also decided that the distinct Victorian air which Amdega designs have about them might be in conflict with the more modern aesthetic of the bungalow, but that if the dentil moulding and the ridge cresting were left off then the structure would be visually compatible with the existing domestic architecture. The result is an interesting example of flexibility in Amdega's design because without these two decorative elements the form of the conservatory becomes that much plainer, and consequently not so allied to any particular historical style. Thus the conservatory is capable of complementing a wider range of architectural styles than would be the case with competing ranges of conservatories where the period flavour is designed into the structure itself.

The conservatory added by Lawrence and his wife, at a cost of about $50 per sq ft (.09sq m) inclusive of pre-erection building work (1986), is not intended primarily as a habitat for cultivating plants. What they required most was a room in which they could enjoy the sun in the surroundings of their magnificent gardens, but without actually sitting outside. The couple derive considerable pleasure from being close to their gardens in this way, and Lawrence has plans to install floodlighting amongst the trees, shrubbery and flower beds so that their garden panorama may also be enjoyed from the conservatory late into the evenings. It means they can virtually sit out in the garden in superior comfort without being subject to the vagaries of British weather.

Although Amdega remains one of a dwindling handful of manufacturers still offering a single-glazed model, Robin and Lawrence chose instead to take advantage of the firm's double-glazed alternative. Blinds, self-regulating roof vents and central heating are not featured in the finished structure. It was not a viable proposition to extend the ducted warm air system in the bungalow out to the conservatory, and some form of electric heating may be installed should it prove necessary. Without blinds, though, the interior of the conservatory is exposed to full sunlight and temperatures have soared well over 100°F (37.8°C) inside. While the owners find this quite tolerable, this kind of heat does prove lethal to insects. Consequently there are heaps of dead species to be found from time to time on shelves, sills and floor which need removing or they become unsightly. For this routine chore Lawrence has discovered the perfect solution – a powerful hand-held rechargeable mini-cleaner which effortlessly vacuums away dust and insect debris.

In common with many fellow purchasers of conservatories, Lawrence and Robin employed their own local builder to put in the base, erect the dwarf walls, set the floor and erect the conservatory. Unfortunately there was an unacceptably long delivery date on supplies of squint bricks for the dwarf walls, so standard bricks were used instead; once finished, these walls were rendered and painted white, so that the whole structure was white thereby emphasising its sense of space, air and light. Despite the fact that ambient temperatures can soar quite spectacularly high, the overall 'whiteness' of the paintwork, together with the terrazzo floor of marble tiles, makes it 'feel' cool within. The effect is something like that achieved by the kind of Moorish architecture encountered in Mediterranean countries. The floor itself, in this instance, did cause some heartache – mainly because of the builder's lack of experience, as it transpired. The marble tiles were laid on a dry base when they should have been set onto a wet surface. Consequently they settled out very unevenly and had to be lifted, then re-set. However, they still remained stubbornly uneven and had to be sanded over and polished down by machine and by hand before they were acceptably level. Obviously this caused no small amount of nuisance to Robin and Lawrence, who were not only deprived of the use of their conservatory during this retrieval work, but who were also faced with the additional inconvenience of a second and third round of on-site working after their conservatory had been put into commission and they had already begun to enjoy its benefits.

CASE STUDY 11

Just as Lawrence and his wife had plans to install flood-lighting in their garden, so also can lighting be employed inside the conservatory to quite dramatic effect, particularly by placing spotlights adjacent to planters and directing them upwards through the leaves thereby creating columns of light around favourite plants. This is a prime night-time feature in a 200sq ft (18sq m) timber conservatory recently added to the home of a retired brigadier and his wife. Both the conservatory and its furnishings were a combined retirement and birthday present from their son, but all the strategic planning and its subsequent execution proceeded like a military campaign under the direction of the brigadier himself.

The brigadier and his wife started out with the intention of creating a 'plant jungle' in which humans could also sit, dine, live and enjoy not only the internal environment, but also the view across the garden. However, this initial concept seemed to put people and plants too much in competition, and was modified towards the idea of a shared space in which they would be in equal partnership. Ultimately this particular conservatory has come to serve as a 'garden, or sun room', to use the brigadier's own words, which accounts for the scale and type of furniture selected, the relationship between human beings and plants, as well as the installation of a comprehensive lighting system. The ceiling lights and the standard lamp were designed and custom-made to fit in with the conservatory's décor. The furniture, essentially of cane material with fabric colours in blues, greens and browns, the mix of terracotta pots and white wood planters, all harmonize with the form and colour of the light shades to complement this carefully designed interior. Furthermore, the sash design in this 16 by 13ft (4.8 by 3.9m) octagonal Amdega model was modified so that the shape of the frames matched those of the house. The house itself, an early nineteenth-century construction and originally a pair of single-storey cottages, is now converted into one dwelling with its exterior walls finished in white. Because his home is situated in a conservation area the brigadier was most concerned to achieve a symbiotic relationship of conservatory with house, in which the former would appear to grow quite naturally out of the latter. His 'garden, or sun room' is also white painted and has an off-white marbled effect floor laid in Amtico tiles. The relationship between the two structures is a complete success.

Although planning permission was not strictly required, it was nonetheless sought. Living in a conservation area, with views across an unspoilt village green, difficulties with local authority planning regulations might have been anticipated. In the event the Cambridge-shire authority made no special conditions.

Ordered in May and delivered on site by July, the structure was erected by an Amdega team on a solid concrete foundation, and brick dwarf walls were put in to Amdega's own general specifications by a firm of builders from the village itself. Such was the accuracy with which the sub-structure was prepared that the erection team had all the structural components in place in one single day, rather than the usual two to three days normally required for similar projects.

Double glazing was specified as a pre-requisite for two main reasons. The owners wished to maintain an ambient temperature of 70°F (21°C) within their conservatory all year round and double glazing reduces heat loss by a factor approaching 40 per cent. They also pointed out their particular need for improved sound insulation and for additional structural rigidity, to help counter the prevailing south-westerly winds that are accelerated by a venturi effect created by the juxtaposition of the brigadier's home with the neighbouring property.

As a former engineer himself, the brigadier planned the siting and erection of his conservatory with the kind of thoroughness one might expect. Heat losses were all carefully calculated beforehand and related to the specified target temperature. So too was the amount of sun to which the conservatory would be subjected, given its north-north-west facing prospect. Unlike so many fellow purchasers, top light screening was ordered at the outset, and additional side-hung venetian blinds with wooden slats were added subsequently. However, when the author visited this conservatory only six months after its completion he was surprised to find that it had no direct access to it from within the house itself. This meant having to walk a few paces across the patio from the rear entrance of the house in order to reach it, something the brigadier readily owned might deter them from using it in poor weather. Recognising this as a shortcoming, a plan was already in hand to remove a living-room window and replace it with a set of double doors opening onto the conservatory. As no throughway into the house had been envisaged in the original plan, so the domestic central-heating system had not been extended to the conservatory; instead, an electrical ring main with numerous outlet sockets had been installed so that independent fan heaters could be used. These remain under thermostatic control (with manual override) thereby allowing flexibility and easy regulation of temperature to the optimum 70°F (21°C).

OPPOSITE

The brigadier's conservatory. A salutory lesson in precise planning resulting in a structure that meets carefully pre-specified conditions.

CASE STUDY 12

The red-brick Victorian house in a sleepy north Bedfordshire village occupied by Helen and Richard has been in Richard's family for three generations. Like the family, the house itself has an interesting history, having been commissioned by the local landed gentry as a shooting lodge for weekend guests. A house in a rural setting such as this, the aspiration of many a putative urban escapee, can bring with it a host of benefits; but never far away will be a new set of problems requiring imaginative solutions if the original character of the place is to be preserved. This however, is precisely the kind of challenge almost anyone would undertake enthusiastically. In the case of Richard and Helen's house each generation of the family has contributed in some way to improving the quality of the dwelling. The main drawback felt by Richard and his wife was a too limited living space, and so their contribution has been to increase the domestic area. It must be something of an irony that the priorities of those Victorian builders were in such contrast to what home owners of the present day are seeking. Outdoors Richard and Helen have space to spare in a superb, mature, landscaped garden which sweeps majestically away from their house down a gentle slope; whereas indoors there is almost a sense of confinement. Cosy, comfortable, but relatively restricted.

Finding both their sitting and dining rooms rather too small, Helen and Richard began considering how they might extend their home without making any major structural alterations. Finally they decided to add a conservatory, thereby capitalising on the abundance of space outside and converting at least some of it to interior space instead. First ideas centred on some form of lean-to glazed structure. But having called in their local Amdega consultant to advise, they quickly realised that the lean-to proposition would be hampered because of insufficient vertical height to upstairs windows as well as by the disposition of doors, windows and downpipes. The alternative was to erect an octagonal conservatory set onto the rear elevation that would provide about 200sq ft (18.5sq m) of floor area and give a vertical height of 11ft 6in (3.5m) to the roof apex. This structure has entrances to it from both the living room and the dining room, there are exits to the patio on its east side, and impressive, special width double doors set into its south end which open onto a flight of stone steps leading to the garden below.

OPPOSITE

Richard and Helen's conservatory borrows from the ample space outdoors to create additional domestic living room.

Figs 37–40 Conservatory
at The Red House

BUILDER TO SUPPLY AND FIX LEAD OR ALUMINIUM FLASHING
TO WALL RAFTERS AND AROUND EXISTING SOIL PIPES.

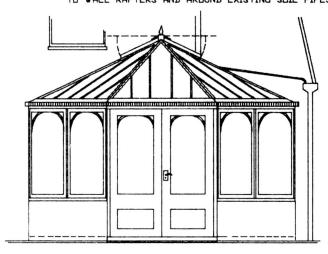

FRONT ELEVATION

WHEN SETTING OUT DWARF WALL, ENSURE
THAT CONSERVATORY UNITS DO
NOT INTERFERE WITH EXISTING WINDOWS.

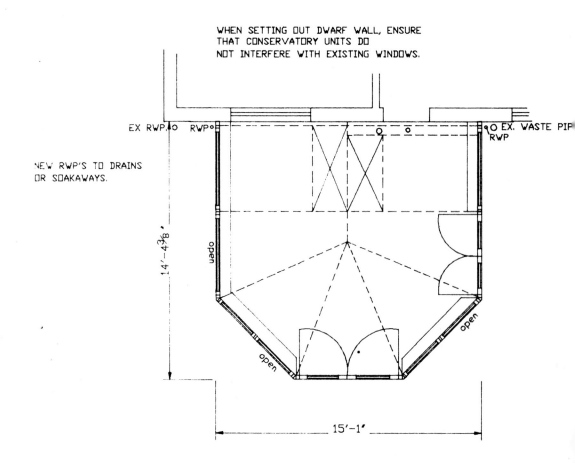

EX RWP. RWP

NEW RWP'S TO DRAINS
OR SOAKAWAYS.

EX. WASTE PIP
RWP

14'-4⅜'

open

open

open

15'-1'

PLAN VIEW

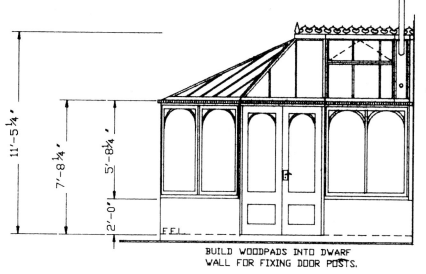

9" PLYWOOD PANEL
TO REAR OF
CONSERVATORY TO
ACCOMODATE EXISTING
SOIL VENT PIPES

BUILD WOODPADS INTO DWARF
WALL FOR FIXING DOOR POSTS.

SIDE ELEVATION

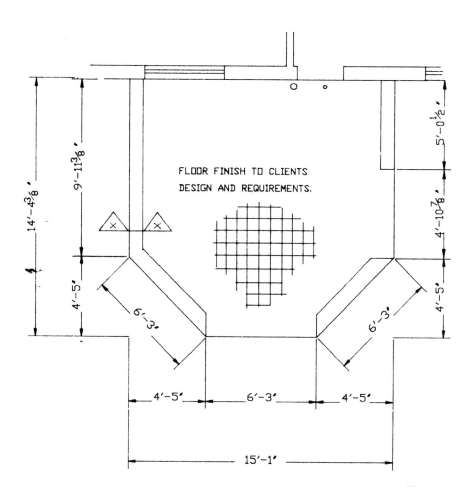

FLOOR FINISH TO CLIENTS
DESIGN AND REQUIREMENTS.

BASEWORK LAYOUT

The result is a captivating, glazed living room with ridge-cresting and dentil-moulding features that mark it out as 'Victorian', perfectly integrating house with garden. Almost 3,000cu ft (843cu m) of additional space has been achieved at an inclusive cost of about £5.50 per cu ft (.03cu m) (1986 prices). In this unit cost assessment the conservatory itself accounts for approximately two thirds of the total, while the remainder has financed materials and the labour associated with site preparation, raising dwarf walls and setting floor blocks. In the preparation work several factors had to be taken into account. For instance, the significant difference in levels between the garden and ground floor of the house had to be overcome, which meant building up the foundations to meet the house level. At the same time access to the rear of the property could only be gained from the front, so every item had to be manhandled through to the site at the back, and this increased labour charges dramatically. Richard and Helen wanted the exposed brick surfaces on the dwarf wall interiors to match the existing weathered Victorian reds of the original external walls – this meant finding a source of bricks contemporary with the originals, reclaiming them and re-cycling them into the project. More expense again, but reckoned to be well justified.

The completed conservatory is fully double glazed and finished in dazzling white. The night-storage radiator system of central heating in the house has been extended to the conservatory to take advantage of the lower off-peak tariff. Not knowing whether one single night storage unit would radiate sufficient heat in the coldest winter months, Richard took the precaution of having a ring main and several 13 amp sockets installed so that additional heating could be brought in if necessary. He and Helen also added three top light roller blinds to the 'A'-frame roof sections to provide sun screening at the south-facing end of the structure. These are made from an unusual acrylic material, regularly perforated and with an apparently metallised finish – and at approximately £100 each (1986) are well worth consideration. These particular blinds are manufactured in the North East and are readily available through Amdega. Finally the flooring, both functional and attractive, consists of slabs of simulated York stone from Marshalls of Halifax.

Featuring a wire snow guard along the edge of the roof above it, the timber framework of this conservatory rests on the outer leaf of the cavity wall leaving the inner leaf to form an ideal support for shelving – a place between floor and ceiling levels to display a few plants. The problem of furnishing and deciding on the most appropriate style still remains under consideration, as Helen and Richard have been experimenting with several different types of plants – they find that oleander, which never once flowered indoors, blooms prolifically in their conservatory: palm, stefanotis and avocado also seem suited to this environment. Abutilon, though it is colourful and grows well, seems to attract too much fly. However, ultimately they both envisage a return to the eighteenth-century citrus tradition with the introduction of lemon and orange plants for colour and form, but most of all for fragrance. Their conservatory would eventually be dedicated to citrus varieties only, and Helen believes this will be sufficient as the space is after all principally for sitting in, dining in, and entertaining in rather than for raising plants.

CASE STUDY 13

Muriel would have liked an Amdega-style conservatory, but she realised that for her modern, semi-detached home a more rectilinear design in aluminium would be more suitable. A visit to her local garden centre – Bickerdikes in Sandy – gave her the opportunity to see several models on display. As a result she was able to decide on one of the Baco range.

Muriel describes her conservatory unequivocally as a sun room. It looks out onto her small, manageable garden enclosed within larch-lap fencing panels that afford some measure of privacy on what is otherwise an open-plan estate. The idea for a conservatory of her own sprang from a holiday in Eastbourne's Hydro Hotel which also boasts a sun room, although on a somewhat grander scale. Muriel's sun room may be rather more modest, even though it does span the full width of her home's rear elevation, but it is no less effective in meeting her requirements. It provides a most relaxing environment, which partly results from the calm green light diffusing the room – this is effected by filtering the sunlight through a layer of tinted sun screening, apparently made from a bubble-polythene sheet of the kind often employed in packaging to absorb the sudden impact of rough handling. It also results from the gentle dry warmth that serves to soothe tight muscles and aching joints. According to Muriel every senior citizen should have a conservatory. This is where she takes the occasional meal, works on the daily newspaper crossword, takes morning coffee or afternoon tea with friends, or, as a lady of mature years herself, just generally enjoys the therapeutic value conferred by her sun room.

This conservatory is appropriately furnished with upholstered tubular steel loungers, tubular-framed circular tables, and huge, bright and cheerful parasols. The furniture – echoing Bauhaus or de Stijl 'modernism' – seems in perfect harmony with the aluminium structure. Square, coloured concrete paving stones serve to emphasise the geometric quality of the entire design experience. These

Muriel relaxing in her Baco conservatory sun room.

structures require only minimum maintenance. And Muriel deliberately keeps inside conservatory chores to a minimum as well. Her one small concession to organic form – a collection of green plants – is contained in a self-watering planter and therefore requires very little attention.

By way of footnote to this particular case study it is worthwhile recording that Muriel's sun room actually foiled an attempted break-in to her home. The intruders were unable to penetrate beyond its toughened glass, or force the lock on its garden side door without disturbing Muriel and her immediate neighbours. Although the structure suffered some minor damage, it remains a convincing demonstration of the claim that a conservatory added to the rear of a property, enclosing the rear entrance and ground floor windows, can indeed raise the level of home security.

CASE STUDY 14

Where Muriel preferred a bright metal finish for her sun room, David and Cynthia opted for a bronzed outer surface to their 16 by 8ft (4.8 by 2.4m) model from the Baco range. This particular aluminium structure perfectly complements their home for two main reasons. Firstly, theirs is a modern house on a young estate, so the visual aesthetic of the conservatory is very much in accord with the prevailing architectural style. Secondly, because Cynthia and her husband are both career-oriented they have little time to devote to gardening. Consequently they have established an Italian garden that requires very little attention, yet is a feature adding interest to the rear of their property. The garden has permanent lighting installed too, so that it may be enjoyed late into the evening. The conservatory looks onto this attractive mini-panorama making the sun room and continental garden mutually complementary.

Although there are a couple of plants in their conservatory – one at each end – David and Cynthia are emphatic that this is not intended as a plant habitat. Pessimistic about the quality of English summers, this 128sq ft (11.52sq m) structure justifies their investment by providing a garden room where they can relax, dine, or entertain outside throughout the year yet be sheltered from the weather. Since it serves primarily as a leisure room, the conservatory is to be fitted with a stereo system and television so as to enhance its recreational potential even further. Unusually, the floor has been carpeted – in a pink pile that colour co-ordinates with the upholstery fabric of the tubular-frame furniture consisting of loungers, dining table and chairs. The carpet not only makes the space feel warmer both psychologically and in actuality, it also improves the acoustic quality of the interior by reducing what is otherwise a noticeable echo. The floor itself has been raised and suspended on blockboard some 3in (7.75cm) above the concrete base in order to prevent damp penetration and subsequent damage.

One of the inherent advantages of these aluminium-framed conservatories is the minimal sitework required and the speed with which they can be assembled. In this case the structure was anchored to a double-height course of bricks and fully erected by an experienced team within two days. Being a modular construction, based on a 49in (112.5cm) standard unit, the design is flexible. This means doors and window components may be arranged at will to suit individual requirements. David took advantage of this to have one door centrally placed, facing approximately south east and opening into the garden, with another at the southern gable end of the lean-to structure giving ready access to the drive and the garage.

The house itself has aluminium window frames and sliding patio-style doors to the front and rear, also in aluminium, which all harmonise with the conservatory, but where the house is double glazed, the leisure room remains single glazed. Although it is not centrally heated, sufficient heat from the ducted warm air system in the house spills into the sun room to keep it comfortably warm. Only in the coldest winter months will it need supplementing with additional heat from a portable source, making it in consequence a space for all seasons. And at something like £17 per sq ft (.09sq m) (1986) these aluminium varieties, just like their timber counterparts, lend themselves to a wide variety of uses and are a continuing source of satisfaction and enjoyment for their owners.

Interior of the Baco conservatory added to their home by David and Cynthia.

OPPOSITE

Above: *From Amdega – a double ended octagonal conservatory linked to the house by a box gutter system and featuring high side framing, MSH/MSR window sashes with a special ship-lap base below the side frames. Finished in natural cedarwood stain.*

Below: *A modular octagonal conservatory by Amdega with a special section erected in a garden at Burford near Oxford. Almost 29ft long and 15ft wide this structure features an unusual internal partition.*

5
Plants for the Conservatory

The tradition of the large, public conservatory or winter garden is essentially Victorian and still enthusiastically preserved in towns and cities throughout the UK. There is, perhaps, nothing more appropriate than to make a visit of discovery to a public conservatory in a town first established in the Victorian era to see what plants, especially house plants, can be successfully cultivated. Middlesbrough in north-east England is one such town, and in many ways epitomises Victorian towns everywhere.

Middlesbrough grew explosively, from being an instant but rationally planned grid-iron town of 5,463 inhabitants, until in the sixty years between 1841 and the turn of the century it had become a bustling urban area of 91,302 inhabitants. The next half-century to 1951 was to see a further 56,034 added to the population. The town owed its prosperity then to a combination of environmental factors which made it an ideal terminus for the Darlington–Stockton Railway's extension to a rivermouth port on the Tees; and also to substantial deposits of local ironstone, which together with limestone from the Pennines and fuel from the nearby Durham coalfields, meant that Middlesbrough – formerly Port Darlington – would become an important centre for iron production and later on for steel. As fast as the prosperity founded on iron- and steel-making grew, so recreational areas that included public parks were designated. Public parks, yes. But by a curious kind of oversight no public conservatory or winter garden. There were, however, a great number of private conservatories – many of them designed and built by W. Richardson & Company of Darlington – and this is perhaps not so surprising as Middlesbrough is only about twelve miles from Darlington. For the most part these private conservatories had been commissioned by middle-class merchants, tradespeople, ironmasters and other industrialists, who had moved out of the original urban centre to reside on the town's more rural, suburban fringes.

One of Middlesbrough's founding fathers was the ironmaster Henry Ferdinand William Bolckow, who, with a partner, established the company of Bolckow & Vaughn in 1841 on a 6 acre (2.4 hectare) site near the river Tees. This foundry, with its forging and rolling mills made castings in brass as well as iron for marine, steam engine and wagon components. By 1853 Henry Bolckow was wealthy enough to commission the building of Marton Hall and took up residence there three years later. In 1868 Bolckow acknowledged the connection between his own Marton Hall residence, the village of Marton close by, and Captain James Cook the eighteenth-century navigator/explorer by dedicating a granite urn to mark the site of Cook's

PREVIOUS PAGE

A modular octagonal ended conservatory fixed to the house by a box gutter.

Conservatories can also provide ideal growing conditions for many kinds of plants and make very elegant greenhouses.

cottage birthplace, which had been demolished precisely a century earlier. H. W. F. Bolckow died in 1878 and forty-five years later in 1923, the Bolckow family decided to bequeathe Marton Hall and its 134-acre (54.2 hectare) estate to Middlesbrough Corporation for use as a public park. This is now known as Stewart Park and contains a substantial 150,000cu ft (42,450cu m) conservatory erected on the site of Bolckow's former private conservatory, which had been demolished along with Marton Hall itself early in 1960.

Today, Middlesbrough's Stewart Park conservatory – completed in 1963 – neatly encapsulates a number of historical links. It maintains a link with the earlier Victorian tradition of erecting public conservatories and winter gardens, like the Palm House at Kew and the winter gardens in Paris or Berlin. Appropriately enough this modern conservatory in Middlesbrough owes its existence to the personal wealth of an entrepreneurial Victorian industrialist, himself concerned with the production and exploitation of iron. This of course was the most important basic material of his age, that lent itself to pre-fabricated building operations, which in turn made possible that ultimate conservatory known as the Crystal Palace. The Stewart Park conservatory also acknowledges Captain James Cook, and features a special section containing plants native to the lands discovered during the navigator's several voyages.

In design the Stewart Park conservatory is essentially a rectangle measuring 139ft (42.25m) by 43ft (13.07m) running east to west. However, there are central entrance vestibules, originally intended as aviaries, on the north and south sides of this rectangle, which serve to give it a cruciform shape reminiscent of church architecture. The conservatory was erected to a design by W. Richardson & Company of Darlington (now known as Amdega Limited) and realised in steel, which is entirely appropriate in view of Middlesbrough's iron- and steel-making heritage. As a pre-fabricated structure with curvilinear steelwork trusses surmounted by a lantern roof some 25ft (7.6m) high, this was designed as a very functional building. Its form is clean, crisp and hard-edged giving it an almost clinically sharp appearance. The ground plan of the structure specified a highly formalised and absolutely symmetrical arrangement of four central palm beds, two on either side of a circular pool area. The space within the conservatory is divided into three separate sections, which today provide environments for sub-tropical, temperate, and Captain Cook specimens. The conservatory's sub-tropical zone is both hot and humid, with temperatures kept constantly at around 70°F (21°C), and a high level of humidity maintained by dampening the footpath area two to four times a day. The central, temperate zone has a regular temperature of between 55°F (13°C) and 60°F (18.5°C), is less humid and is generally left with ventilation on overnight. Meanwhile, the specialist Cook species' zone is marginally warmer than its neighbouring temperate section, but receives less ventilation.

The sub-tropical habitat at the west end of the conservatory contains some thirty plant species, which are listed alphabetically below. Also listed are thirty-three species from the temperate habitat and a further twenty species from the Captain Cook collection. In addition, there are a number of plants, cacti and succulents from the vestibules. Of this collection, some are not suitable for the domestic conservatory, but the majority should be easy to cultivate and would only serve to enhance either the modern-or traditional-style home conservatory.

Plants displayed in the sub-tropical section are:

Anthurium	Cinnamon Plant	Pilea
Banana Palm	Dieffenbachia	Peperomia
Begonia	Dracaena	Philodendron
Bread-fruit Tree	*Ficus lyrata*	Sago Plant
Cheese Plant	Fittonia	Sansevieria
Codaeium	Hibiscus	Spathiphyllum
Croton	Kentia Palm	Stephanotis
Cordyline	Monstera	Tenanthia
Clerodendrum	Nidularium	Tradescantia
Columnea		

As part of his day-to-day running of the Stewart Park conservatory the gardener manages a substantial area where plants are presented as a living sculpture, using their varying qualities of form, shape, colour, texture, mass and scale in sensitively designed displays that are expressed in terms of vertical, horizontal and inclined planes. The gardener achieves this by using ground-level plant beds, by suspending plants above head-height in baskets, and by growing potted plants on benches on the intermediate level. The total effect produces a richly coloured, three-dimensional panorama in which the art of the gardener has been carefully camouflaged, but the visitor's careful scrutiny is repaid if he discovers how it is all achieved. A guided tour of Middlesbrough's public conservatory, so much appreciated by town residents and visitors alike, provides an opportunity to look at individual plants, small groups of plants thoughtfully juxtaposed, and larger banks of plants collected together – all intended to achieve particular effects.

One of the peperomias in the sub-tropical section is known as *variegata* – a favourite in the conservatory gardener's displays. This is one of two variegated forms of *peperomia magnifolia* which originates from San Domingo. As *variegata* matures its creamy-coloured leaves turn to a light green. Placed on either side of this central plant with its ascending stems, are potted trailing ivies – in this instance *hedera helix* Glacier – which act as a counterbalance in the way they grow down from the bench. Glacier is one of more than a dozen hardy evergreen trailers and has small green-grey leaves with highlighted white edges. Again, by way of a change in composition, the *peperomia variegata* is teamed with a silver *begonia rex*. *Begonia rex* is a rhizatomous plant originally from Assam – begonias seem to prefer well lit areas, but need to be sited out of direct sunlight. Forming a group with the peperomia and the *begonia rex* – as part of a much larger bench display – a chlorophytum or spider plant nicely fills in the area behind. Native to South Africa, chlorophytum must be one of the easiest plants to cultivate and propagate. It appears to have an excellent tolerance to widely differing conditions and requires minimal attention. The plant has long lanceolate green and white leaves – from within these it produces stems bearing small plantlets, which readily root and then grow on independently. With *peperomia variegata* and *begonia rex* in the foreground and chlorophytum in the mid-ground, this small, five-plant group is completed by a codaeium and a fern placed in the background. The codaeium, a member of the croton family, is also from South Africa. Both the broad- and thin-leaved varieties love warm, humid conditions. With the codaeium humidity is most important, so in a domestic conservatory frequent hand-spraying is essential as the plant is particularly prone to attack by red spider if it is allowed to become too dry. The fern selected to fill in the backdrop in this display is a thin-leafed fern known as *asparagus meysii* and is one of some 300 asparagus varieties.

An hisbiscus flower is well worth looking at in isolation. (The moisture droplets on this particular specimen indicate that it needs regular spraying to maintain an appropriate level of humidity.) Stewart Park's conservatory chooses *hibiscus trionum*, which derives from Africa, for its sub-tropical habitat. More commonly known as the 'flower-of-an-hour', this particular hibiscus is very showy, but shortlived as its name would suggest. The flowers themselves are strikingly beautiful, very luscious and sensuous with their creamy-yellow petals surrounding and seeming to swallow the darker maroon centres. *Hibiscus trionum* also appears in creamy white, but whatever the colour the delicate nature of the flower itself always contrasts nicely with the more rugged appearance of its leaves. Also selected for individual attention is *pilea cadlierei*, frequently referred to as the aluminium plant thanks to the appearance of its leaves. Pilea is an evergreen perennial that really does lend itself to use as a foliage plant and is worth cultivating in the home conservatory for that reason. *Pilea cadlierei* comes from Vietnam and boasts dark-green leaves veined with silver – hence the name aluminium plant. The plant grows well enough even in a poorly lit situation, but needs ample watering during its growing season.

Some of the plants displayed in this Middlesbrough conservatory would almost certainly be unsuitable for a domestic conservatory, principally because of the height they can grow to and the amount of space they occupy when spread more fully as mature plants. Occupying the sub-tropical floor beds are banana plants, palms and Swiss cheese plants, which reach to the full 25ft (7.6m) height of the conservatory's lantern roof. *Monstera deliciosa*, the Swiss cheese plant that paradoxically originates in Mexico, is a popular household plant, but easily tops 20ft (6.09m) if unchecked and can have individual leaves with a surface area of some 8sq ft (0.74sq m). Carefully controlled, though, the Swiss cheese plant is viable in the home conservatory, but limiting its growth is a disadvantage as it will then rarely flower. The fully grown and mature plant produces a fascinating pale creamy-yellow flower reminiscent of an arum lily in form, which contains at its centre a stubby, cucumber-like, pale green, pulpy fruit.

The nidularium thrives in this particular conservatory and is used either in bench displays, or in the sub-tropical section's central bed beneath the palms, banana plants and cheese plants, – this environment with its accompanying warmth and humidity must be close to the nidularium's native climate, which is the tropical rain-forest of Brazil. The nidularium belongs to the bromeliad group – or pineapple plant family – and apart from its bracts that turn pink during flowering, the plant also produces tubular flowers that can be blue, white, or more occasionally can be yellow.

Another striking hibiscus is a pink-flowering type whose leaves are strongly reminiscent of the *hibiscus rosa-sinensis* that features double flowers. In its specific setting in the Stewart Park conservatory this plant provides an eye-catching splash of sudden colour among the dark green leaves of the moranta and small palm by which it is surrounded and overshadowed.

Perhaps one of the most impressive sub-tropical plants is the anthurium. It is commonly known as the 'painter's palette' thanks to its distinctive palette-shaped flower, with its long spadix resembling the thumb of the hand holding the palette. This plant is native to Colombia, and can grow anything up to 18in (45.7cm) high; it normally blooms from spring onwards into late summer, its flowers a strident red colour. In this particular conservatory the anthurium is grouped with four other plants all of which complement and contrast dynamically with one another because of the visual rhythms created by their varied forms and colours. Beneath the *anthurium andreanum* a spathiphyllum, which also comes from Colombia, has been carefully placed. With its bright, shiny lanceolate leaves this particular specimen, *spathiphyllum wallisii* (rather than the very similar-looking hybrid variety *spathiphyllum X manna loa*) creates a finely balanced relationship with its South American cousin. The spathiphyllum and the anthurium are related species, but the *spathiphyllum wallisii* is more easily grown and consequently is the more popular. This plant is often called 'white sails' because its white and waxy vertical spathe does evoke the image of a wind-filled spinnaker. These two plants need regular hand-spraying to maintain an appropriate level of humidity and also require adequate warmth. Positioned to the rear, side and front of the painter's palette and white sails are a dracaena, a peperomia and a begonia. The selected peperomia is *peperomia magnoliifolia*, originating in San Domingo, the green-gold variety whose leaves have distinctive cream edging. In the foreground of the group, and positioned so that it falls gently away from the spathiphyllum is a *begonia glaucophylis*, which is pink when in flower.

Another delightful grouping is achieved by juxtaposing dracaena, palm, peperomia, maranta and codiaeum: this evokes a real feeling of the lush, sub-tropical environment typical of Malaysia, South America or Africa, all emphasized by the heat and the glistening moisture on flowers and leaves.

Four other plants combine equally dramatically in this sub-tropical habitat. The pineapple plant, or *ananas comosus*, is a soil-based bromeliad. *Ananas comosus* is commercially grown elsewhere for its pineapple fruit, but was imported to the UK in the early years of the eighteenth century. It is very similar in appearance to *ananas sagenaria*, which also sports creamy-white margined leaves with

The pineapple plant, or ananas comosus.

saw-toothed edges. While *ananas comosus* has blue flowers, *sagenaria* has red; both originate in Brazil. Anthurium and maranta help make up the rest of the group.

Banana palm, or *musa cavendishii* is suitable for cultivation in domestic conservatories, but requires ample living room. In season the palm displays fascinating deep purple bracts enclosing clusters of long flowers, which are followed by bunches of banana fruit. These, however, should be regarded as decorative rather than edible. Unless the environmental conditions are near perfect the bananas frequently taste too bitter to be enjoyed. Accompanying the tall banana palm is an equally tall *ficus lyrata* – commonly called the 'fiddle back fig' – that comes from West Africa. Normally a potted specimen would not achieve a growth of much more than 4ft (1.22m). Here, though, (seen here) planted in a bed, the ficus reaches up to more than 15ft (4.56m). Also making use of the upper level space are hanging baskets. Four varieties of columnea are popular plants for suspended displays because of their attractive, eye-catching flowers: *columnea microphylla* and *columnea gloriosa* are both native to Costa Rica; *columnea shiedeana* comes from Mexico. The appealingly sinuous stems of these various columnea plants can reach down to 6ft (1.83m) in length showing scarlet, orange, or orange-scarlet flowers depending on the variety planted.

The central area of the Stewart Park conservatory is maintained as a temperate zone. Among the plants displayed in this temperate area are:

Abutilon	Chrysanthemum	Funiberus
Asparagus Fern	Coleus	Geranium
Asplenium Fern	Cordyline	Ginger Plant
Bamboo	Date Palm	*Hedera helix*
Begonia Rex	Eucalyptus	Irisine
Begonia	Exacum	Lemon Citrus
semperflorens	Fan Palm	Nepeta
Beloperone	Fatsia	Nethrolepsis Fern
Browallia	*Ficus benjamina*	Plectranthus
Celosia	*Ficus pacyfillia*	Reseda
Chlorophytum	Fig Bush	Tomato Tree

The central feature of this section is its ornamental pond, and looking northwards is a bench display of chrysanthemums and fuchsias which form a colourful backdrop. Around the pond's blind side are bamboo plants and arum lilies, *zantedeschia aethiopica*, with their graceful curving flowers and distinctive yellow spadixes. These lilies originate in South Africa and are considered as half-hardy perennials. The aethiopica variety – one of maybe half a dozen or so – can reach between 18 and 36in (45 and 90cm) and flowers between Easter and the early summer. Looking southwards affords a pleasant view of the gently playing fountain which sprinkles the water-surface and helps aereate the pond for the benefit of its fish population. As well as the bamboo plants – or more formally the arundinaria from Japan and China – is a large cupressus, both of which are unsuitable for cultivation in the domestic conservatory because of the space they need; also included in this pond area group is a yellow jasmine, *jasminum nudiflorum*, which has been trained along rustic railings, a winter-flowering plant that needs some form of permanent support. The plant is Chinese in origin, and given the right conditions it will reach up to 10ft (3.04m). Although it is a hardy specimen it can be damaged by cold draughts. The cordyline or cabbage palm is also suitable for a pond area display, and in this particular conservatory the gardener has opted for the *cordyline indivisa* which has long, narrow pointed leaves. *Cordyline indivisa* is a New Zealand species that can reach heights of up to 20ft (6.09m) and spans of 6ft (1.83m); it produces clusters of globular, purple berries in the autumn. While it can grow tall, *cordyline indivisa* is easily restricted to a 4ft (1.22m) ceiling

The shrimp plant, or belloperone guttata *(centre) with* centaurae *(left),* coleus *and* ficus elastica decora, *or india rubber plant (rear).*

if it is potted up. Fatsia is another plant that seems to harmonise well with a waterside environment. Fatsia, native to Japan – hence *fatsia japonica* – has large, rich glossy leaves which will spread anything up to 12ft (3.64m) and therefore cover significantly large areas. October will normally see *fatsia japonica* in bloom with flowering white panicles between 9 and 11 inches (22.8 and 27.9cm) in length.

One attractive composition of these temperate plants has the shrimp plant, or *belloperone guttata* from Mexico placed at its centre. Kept in a temperate and well ventilated environment the shrimp plant can be expected to continue flowering almost indefinitely. *Belloperone guttata* has fairly unobtrusive white flowers at the tips of its pinkish, scale-like bracts. In front and to the left of the shrimp plant a centaurea with its silvery foliage provides a contrast. Alongside it a coleus spreads quantities of leafy colour, while to the rear of the group a tall *ficus elastica decora* – the India-rubber plant from tropical Asia – helps balance the composition vertically.

Looking towards the east end of this Stewart Park conservatory it is just possible to see the section featuring plant species which are associated with the eighteenth-century voyages of Captain James Cook. However, still in the temperate zone a colourful bench display particularly noticed by the visitor is one which contains a wide variety of plants, all carefully chosen and raked back in ascending height until they reach the south-facing glass wall. In this rich and varied arrangement plants have been selected to trail down from the bench as well as to grow up from it. The conservatory gardener has made full use of different plant characteristics and their capacity for vertical and horizontal growth that allows him to organise the conservatory's inner space to achieve particular effects. Helping to define the space vertically is a *physalis aklekengi franchetii* – a Chinese lantern, or bladder cherry plant. Actually it comes from Japan, and can grow to become 2ft (0.609m) tall. Its white flowers – around July – succeed to orangey fruits encased within a delightful red/orange 'rice paper' bladder. These ripen by early autumn. As well as *physalis alkekengi franchetii* gigantea, there is also a smaller variety available called *nana*. Along the aisle are several hanging baskets, which mean that living colour can easily be introduced at many different levels.

If small is beautiful then the charming little *exacum affine* (seen below) is certainly worth a closer look. Its purple flowers with their eye-catching yellow centres are pleasingly fragrant and will normally bloom from July through the summer and on into September. *Exacum* is a compact, bushy kind of plant that will spread to cover an area of about 3sq ft (0.27sq m) around its pot or bed. Two plants that seem to work particularly well together are appropriately pigmented cockscombs and primulas. A cockscomb, or *celosia argentea cristata*, is quite striking in the way it can deliver a sudden splash of colour to predominantly green surrounding foliage. The patterns traced by the wandering edges of this plant's flower crests are no less remarkable than its sudden shock of colour. The particular variety favoured at the Middlesbrough conservatory is called 'jewel box' – as well as the strident red hue, jewel box is also available in yellow and orange. Where cockscomb might be the comedian in the partnership, the primula plays the straight man. Placed behind its partner, the primula's delicate pastel colouring – pink in this instance – simultaneously complements and contrasts with the louder celosia.

Dominating almost one half of another interesting and very varied arrangement is a cordyline while to its left, in a benched display, is a mixed collection of chrysanthemums, coleus and irisine which surround a kind of ficus – the *ficus carica*, or fig tree, which comes from Syria. Figs will grow and fruit in conservatories in the UK providing they are positioned in south-facing aspects. Another display which relies on seven different plants presents a pleasing blend of colour and form that seems to work particularly well: commencing at the back and against the Parisian blind, the group features an air-layered ficus, or India-rubber plant; below this are irisine, browalia, primula, chlorophytum and *hedera helix*, with a small begonia placed in the foreground. At ground level, there is an equally successful mixed group comprising a Colombian *browalia speciosa*, a chlorophytum, a *begonia fuchsioides* from Brazil with its wealth of bright red flowers, and an irisine, which the gardener here frequently employs as a 'spot' plant when he needs to throw in a sudden splash of colour to liven up foliage that is predominantly green. One plant in this particular conservatory, always pointed out by visitors, is a so-called 'tomato tree'. An excursion to the conservatory in autumn will see this tomato tree in fruit. However, these prove to be essentially decorative because, like the bananas, they have an exceptionally bitter taste. The bitterness is, though, ascribed by the staff to inappropriate soil conditions in its present location; the fruit should in fact be edible.

An especially colourful display is created by bringing a variety of benched pot plants together – chiefly chrysanthemums, coleus, ivy, fern and begonia. The chrysanthemums favoured for this setting belong to the UK species of *chrysanthemum parthenium* – one is a pink variety named 'Maid Marion', another, a red variety known as 'lipstick'. All four chrysanthemums – pink, red, white and yellow – are perennials with long-lasting flowers; this particular species prefers well drained soil and a sunny position. The ornamental leaves of the several coleus in this display are unmistakably those of *coleus blumei* coming from Java. Altogether, there are well over 100 different species of this perennial – a plant, incidentally, that is easily propagated from cuttings. Coleus plants can be kept quite bushy by pinching out any small flowers which may appear; their richly diverse leaves, always reminiscent of large nettles in shape, come in an almost inexhaustible variety of reds, greens, yellows and maroons. The *celosia argentea* and *celosia plumosa* chosen here have unusually distinctive red and yellow colouration, and a common ivy, *hedera helix*, found almost anywhere in Europe, makes very useful ground or trailing cover. Begonias are particularly suitable for domestic conservatories and may be divided into rhizone, tuber and fibrous-rooted types: the first is grown especially for its ornamental leaves, while tuberous begonias are noted for their flowers, as are the evergreen fibrous types. Chrysanthemum, coleus and ivy can be enlivened by the addition of browalia and exacum. The South American *browalia speciosa* makes a fine pot plant with its 2in (5cm) wide, violet-blue flowers, and like the delightful little *exacum affine* lends itself particularly well to conservatory conditions. The dainty, bushy exacum, from the island of Socotra in the Indian Ocean, bears yellow-centred, five-pointed purple flowers; it will normally flower from early summer to early autumn and will spread out to cover a 12in (30cm) span.

Internal view of an Amdega double glazed modular/special conservatory comprising 12ft 1in × 13ft 6in long octagonals on either side of a 9ft 11in wide lean-to section. Designed for a house at Weybridge, Surrey, this single glazed example features such optional extras as MSS sashes, ridge cresting and denil moulding.

A final display in the temperate section is arranged with an interesting juxtaposition of colour, form and texture: a *belloperone guttata*, or shrimp plant, is placed alongside a ficus; below these two are first a coleus, then a senecio, which is frequently and more commonly known as cineraria. There are several names – senecio bicolor, senecio cineraria and cineraria bicolor – for this particular silvery-leafed and silvery-stemmed plant, which owes its unusual appearance to thousands of fine white hairs on both leaf and stem. Senecio produces yellow flowers from mid-summer to early autumn.

It is frequently pleasing to gardeners to design displays in a conservatory, either public or domestic, around some kind of central theme. In Middlesbrough's Stewart Park conservatory the gardeners have seized the opportunity to exploit the Park's associations with the celebrated explorer James Cook. Cook was native to the nearby village of Marton, which is now a Middlesbrough suburb, and his

This double glazed conservatory measures 12ft 1in × 15ft 10½in long and is in Wootton-Underwood, near Aylesbury

achievements are commemorated in an award-winning museum sited alongside the conservatory. Regarded as one of the greatest maritime explorers, this eighteenth-century seaman made a number of voyages across and around the Pacific Ocean, discovering not only Australia and New Zealand but also several individual islands and island groups. While the neighbouring Cook Museum celebrates the captain's discoveries by means of audio-visual media and displays, the conservatory commemorates his exploits by displaying specimens of the plant species native to the lands he claimed for the future British Empire.

The Captain Cook section has a temperature slightly higher than the temperate section adjacent to it, but enjoys less ventilation; it houses the following plants:

Arum lily	Cabbage palm	Maiden hair fern
Aurellia	Canaryensis	Norfolk Island pine
Begonia rex	Eussissus	Orchid
(fireflush)	*Fatshedria liziae*	Pineapple lily
Bilbergia windii	*Grevillea banksii*	Stag-horn fern
Bird of paradise	Holly fern	Zinzibar
Bottlebrush	*Machydamia*	
	termifolia	

Among these specimens is the curious Australian bottlebrush, or callistemon. Although possibly too large to contemplate for average-sized domestic conservatories unless curbed by careful pruning, the callistemon is nonetheless quite striking, especially when it displays its bottlebrush blooms which consist of small flowers with either yellow or scarlet centres. Behind the callistemon, an example of kentia palm has been planted – this plant is also known as *howeia palmae foresteriania* in recognition of its origins in the forests of the Lord Howe Islands situated in the Pacific Ocean off the east coast of New South Wales. In general the display in this section is less concerned about grouping or pairing plants for particular effects. Instead the visitor is encouraged to appreciate individual plants like the delicate *brunfelsia pauciflora calycina*, known more popularly as the 'yesterday-today-tomorrow flower'. This plant originates from Brazil (Cook visited the eastern seaboard of South America in 1763) and gains its common name from the fact that its fragrant violet flowers fade to white in discreet, but discernible stages over a forty-eight hour period when the bloom is white for 'yesterday', pale violet

An Amdega conservatory provides an attractive entrance to a house with plenty of colourful plants on display.

for 'today' and an emergent darker violet colour for 'tomorrow'. No horticultural celebration of Cook's achievements could be complete without a eucalyptus tree because of his connections with Australia. The Stewart Park conservatory has a round-leaved variety known as *eucalyptus perviniana* found originally in Australia's New South Wales territory, in Victoria and also Tasmania. One variety of the kentia palm has already been mentioned. However, the aforementioned *howeia foresteriana* is quite difficult to distinguish from the *howeia belmoreana*: the latter has more leaves which are straighter, while the leaves of *foresteriana* tend to droop slightly and are less dense – but both varieties easily reach heights of up to 10ft (3.04m) and will spread to cover an 8sq ft (0.74sq m) area. As well as its kentia palms, this section has examples of the South African arum lily, the *zantedeschia aethiopica*. Arum lilies are noted for their voluptuous white spathes, usually around 6in (15cm) long, which swirl into a central yellow spadix.

The north-west vestibule of the conservatory houses azalea, camellia, chrysanthemum, columnea, fuchsia and primula, and tends to highlight different displays on a more seasonal basis. Cacti and succulents are popular conservatory plants too, and although perhaps no domestic conservatory would be devoted exclusively to them, they monopolize the south-east vestibule of Middlesbrough's public conservatory and occupy a floor area equivalent to many an entire home conservatory. Given sufficient space these plants can easily achieve heights and spreads that will rival anything seen in those American and Spanish desert backdrops essential to that genre of film known as 'the Western'. Cacti can be attractive and do actually bloom on a regular basis; however, unless they are given sufficient space to reach their mature size some may never flower at all. The tallest of the cacti at Stewart Park are the bishop's cap and the bishop's mitre, both of which are respectively six- and four-rib variants of *astrophytum myriostigma*. *Astrophytum myriostigma* itself is the six- (occasionally five-) ribbed cactus – bishop's cap – while *astrophytum myriostigma quadricostatum* is the four-ribbed bishop's mitre. Another tall variety of cactus is the tree type opuntia, with cylindrical stems. At a lower level can be seen the more familiar prickly pear cactus *opuntia scheerii* from Mexico, with bluish-green pear-shaped pads which produce orange-red flowers at their tips. Lower still, and probably more easily managed in domestic conservatories where space may be an important consideration, *agave americana marginata* with its creamy-yellow-edged leaves grows well. However, waiting for it to flower could be considered a lifetime's occupation. Sometimes known as the century plant, this particular succulent can take between twenty and fifty years before it is mature enough to produce its flower, which eventually emerges from the centre of the leaf cluster.

Further Reading

Benton, T. & C. with Sharp, D., *Form and Function* (Crosby Lockwood Staples in association with Open University Press, 1975)

Curl, James Stevens, *Victorian Architecture: Its Practical Aspects* (David & Charles, 1973)

Directory of Garden Chemicals (11th ed, British˙ Agrochemicals Association, 1986)

Fisher, D., *Home Extensions and Conservatories* (David & Charles, 1985)

Hix, John, *The Glass House* (Phaidon Press, 1971)

Kurth, Heinz & Geneste, *Greenhouses for longer summers* (Batsford, 1982)

McGrath, R., & Frost, A. C., *Glass in Architecture and Decoration* (The Architectural Press, 1961)

Taylor, Jasmine (ed), *Conservatories and Garden Rooms* (Macdonald, 1985)

Toogood, Alan, *The Conservatory for Plants and People* (Ward Lock, 1985)

Conservatory Manufacturers

Mr Anthony McGlyne
Commercial Manager
Edenlite
Alusuisse Extruded Products
 Limited
Wern Works
Briton Ferry
Neath
West Glamorgan SA11 2JS
(0639 822677)

Amdega Limited
Faverdale
Darlington
Co Durham DL3 0PW
(0325 468522)

Anglian Home Extensions
40 Chastilian Road
Dartford
Kent DA1 3JL
(0322 92127)

BACO Leisure Products Limited
Freepost
Huntingdon
Cambridgeshire PE18 7EH

Banbury Homes & Gardens
 Limited
Dept CC 0208
PO Box 17
Banbury
Oxfordshire OX17 3NS
(0295 811196)

Mr Alexander Bartholomew
Alexander Bartholomew
 Conservatories
277 Putney Bridge Road
London SW15 2PT
(01 785 7263)

Crittal Warmlife Limited
Freepost
Witham
Essex CM8 3AW
(Freefone 100)

Hadrian Conservatories
Number Eight
Button Mill Estate
Bridgend
Stonehouse
Gloucestershire
(045 382 6459)

Mr Francis Machin
Managing Director
Machin Conservatories
4 Avenue Studios
Sydney Close
London SW3 6HW
(01 350 1581/01 589 7551)

Marston & Langinger
Hall Staithe
Fakenham
Norfolk NR21 9BW
(0328 3067)

Mr Ken Beck
Commercial Manager
New England Conservatories
    Limited
Dept 1H/946
Whitney Road
Daneshill
East Basingstoke RG24 0NS
(0256 468896)

Robinsons of Winchester Limited
Robinson House
Winnall
Winchester SO23 8LH
(0962 61917)

Mr G. M. Burton
Commercial Manager
Room Outside Limited
Goodwood Gardens
Waterbeach
Chichester
West Sussex
(0243 776563)

Turner Conservatories Limited
94 Morehampton Road
Dublin 4
(Workshop & Showroom at:
Fumbally Works
Blackpitts
Dublin 8
(0001 7191888/686688)

Wessex Conservatories
Wessex Aluminium Limited
Unit 8 Wyndham Road
Hawksworth Industrial Estate
Swindon
Wiltshire SN2 1EJ

White Diamond Conservatories
42 South Street
Stanground
Peterborough
(0733 41850)

Useful Addresses

Bovingdon Brickworks Limited
Ley Hill Road
Bovingdon
Hemel Hempstead
Herts
(0442 833176)

The Cane Furniture
2 St James Street
Walthamstow
London E17
(01 520 4606)

Classic Garden Furniture
Audley Avenue
Newport
Shropshire TF10 7DS
(0952 813311)

The Gentle Gardener
Pots and Planters
Gardiner House
Broomhill Road
London SW18

Grosfillex Garden Furniture (UK)
    Limited
10 Chandos Road
London NW10 6NF

Seaton Howard Limited
Independent Conservatory
    Consultants
1 High Street
Yeldon
Bedfordshire
(093 34 53607)

Marshalls (paving and walling)
Southowram
Halifax HX3 9SY

Marston & Langinger
    (Conservatory Accessories)
20 Bristol Gardens
Little Venice
London W9 2JQ
(01 286 7643)

D. S. Prigmore (recycled building
    materials)
Mill Cottage
Mill Lane
Colmworth
Bedfordshire
(023062 264)

Rokes (Stonework garden
    furniture)
Andoversford
Cheltenham GL54 5RJ
(04515 413)

Acknowledgements

I wish to acknowledge the invaluable assistance of Ken Holliday and Peter Cawdell of Amdega Limited, who provided a wealth of advice and information.

I must thank my friend Geoffrey Grant, Lecturer in History of Art and Design at Cleveland College of Art & Design, and former colleagues in the college's Research and Information Unit for help in preparing this book.

I must express my gratitude to Peter Whelan of Cleveland Publicity Services Limited for his assistance with and enthusiasm for the project.

I must also record my thanks to Cleveland County Parks Department for help in preparing the section on conservatory plants.

Finally I should like to thank all of the manufacturers who extended their co-operation to me, and I must thank especially all of those owners who kindly welcomed me into their homes to discuss their conservatories with them.

Without the generous assistance of these various individuals and organisations this book would not have been possible. I can only hope that in writing it I have done justice to all of those who have helped me.

Index